THE FURNESS RAILWAY

RAILWAY

Volume 1

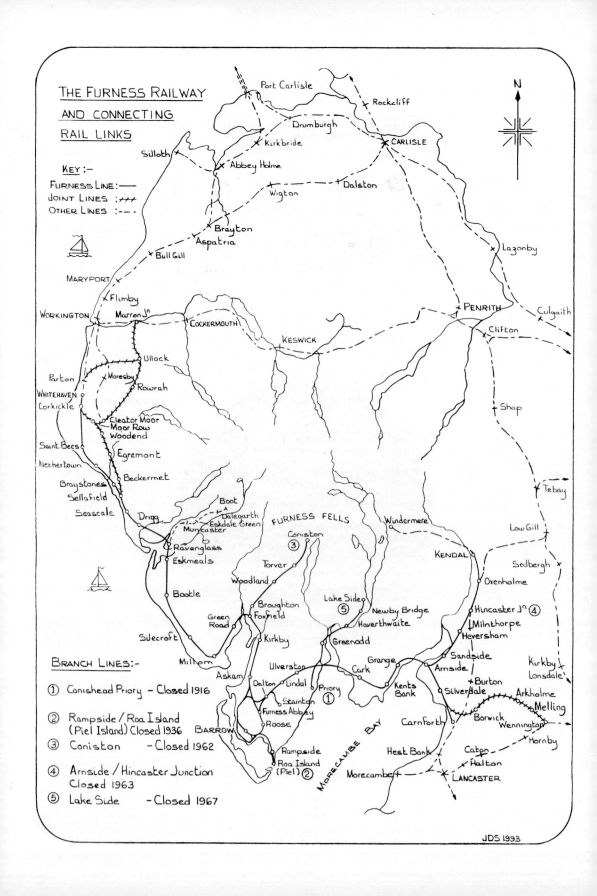

· MEMORIES OF LAKELAND ·

THE FURNESS RAILWAY

An illustrated record including photographs from the Sankey Collection

Volume 1
The line described

K. J. Norman

·RAILWAY HERITAGE·
from
The NOSTALGIA Collection

First published in a single volume as *The Furness Railway* in 1994
New two-volume paperback edition with additional material first published 2001

British Library Cataloguing in Publication Data

A catalogue record for this book is available from the British Library.

ISBN 1 85794 145 4

Silver Link Publishing Ltd
The Trundle
Ringstead Road
Great Addington
Kettering
Northants NN14 4BW

Tel/Fax: 01536 330588
email: sales@nostalgiacollection.com
Website: www.nostalgiacollection.com

Printed and bound in Great Britain

Unless otherwise credited, all photographs are © the Sankey Collection, and the numbers following their captions are the negative numbers. Cumbrian Railway Association negative numbers are also given; requests for prints from both Collections may be made via the Publisher, quoting the relevant numbers.

A Silver Link book
from
The NOSTALGIA Collection

ACKNOWLEDGEMENTS

Grateful thanks are due to Cait Faulkner for invaluable assistance with the drudgery of typing; Phil Cousins of P. R. Design, Barrow, for scanning the initial typescript; Mike Faulkner for the very fine station drawings and for checking the text; Jeff Sankey for producing an excellent map; while special thanks must go to Geoff Holme, not only for careful checking of the captions, but also for giving so generously of his time in the preparation of the text for the publisher. Without his help it would have been much more difficult to produce this book.

Special thanks to Raymond Sankey for his encouragement with the project, and for granting unlimited access to his wonderful collection of photographic negatives.

For the new edition the Sankey Collection photographs have been supplemented with illustrations from several other sources, including photographs from the collections of friends W. Anderson, Dr M. J. Andrews, P. R. Cousins, A. L. Headech, G. Holme, T. Owen, K. E. Royall, R. Fisher, the late Commander G. Taylor RCN, the Cumbrian Railways Association (from their Pattinson/Cumbria Library, Kerr, and Walker collections), The Dock Museum, The Barrow Public Library, BAE Systems, and my own collection. Permission to publish these photographs was granted without hesitation and I am truly grateful for that privilege.

I must also acknowledge the valuable information contained in the quarterly Journal of the Cumbrian Railways Association (CRA), which answered queries and provided an abundant source of expert knowledge whenever it was needed.

The new pictures are acknowledged as they appear and negative numbers are provided with Sankey and CRA photographs.

CONTENTS

FURNESS RAILWAYS CAUTION TO TRESPASSERS

PERSONS TRESPASSING UPON THE RAILWAYS BELONGING TO THE FURNESS RAILWAY COMPANY ARE LIABLE TO A PENALTY OF FORTY SHILLINGS UNDER THE FURNESS RAILWAY ACT 1894 AND IN ACCORDANCE WITH THE PROVISIONS OF THE SAID ACT. PUBLIC WARNING IS HEREBY GIVEN TO ALL PERSONS NOT TO TRESPASS UPON THE SAID RAILWAYS.

AUGUST 1894·   BY ORDER.

A cast iron Furness Railway trespass notice. *Geoff Holme collection*

Half title The Furness Railway's coat of arms was derived from the Great Seal of Furness Abbey, which shows the Virgin Mary holding the Infant Jesus in her left hand, while in her right she carries an orb, symbolising her position as Queen of the World. She stands beneath the centre of three pointed arches and is flanked by two shields, each supported by a monk. Each shield is surmounted by sprigs of deadly nightshade, relating to the Valley of Beckansgill, known locally as the Vale of the Deadly Nightshade, in which the Abbey was built, and there are further sprigs of the plant on either side of the Virgin Mary.

The right-hand shield bears the three lions of England, that on the left is charged with those of Lancaster, and in the lower compartment is the figure of a Wyvern, a mythical creature taking the form of a two-legged dragon.

Encircling the great Seal of the Abbey is the Latin inscription meaning 'The Common Seal of St Mary's of Furness', and the railway company's crest is girdled in gilt lettering, with the company name in the upper portion, beneath which is its motto 'Cavendo Tutus', meaning 'Secure by Caution'. This was also the motto of the Cavendish family, the local Lords of the Manor, whose head was such a valuable sponsor of the Furness Railway Company in its formative years.

THE SANKEY COLLECTION

Towards the end of the 19th century Edward Sankey, a master printer who had established a printing company in Barrow, began to take photographs of subjects suitable for sale as picture postcards, which he started to produce in large quantities. He travelled widely in Cumberland, Westmorland and the Furness District of Lancashire and beyond for his pictures, which, fortunately for the railway-lovers of today, often included a photograph of the railway station in the places he visited. A reputation as a commercial photographer was soon established, resulting in his appointment as an official Furness Railway photographer in about 1906.

During the summer he sailed daily on the cross-bay paddle-steamers taking pictures of the passengers, and the steamers gave him easy access to Blackpool, Fleetwood and the adjacent Fylde villages, all of which were extensively recorded by his camera. The Sankey collection of photographs eventually consisted of more than 15,000 half-plate negatives, many of them on glass plates, covering all aspects of the contemporary scene – shipping using the port of Barrow; vessels, naval and commercial, built at the local shipyard; airships; trams and buses; early motor vehicles; street scenes; events; and pictorial views in the surrounding villages, the nearby Lake District, the Fylde and beyond. Nearly 8,000 of these negatives still exist, including more than 300 of railway interest, and it is from the latter that many of the illustrations for this book have been selected.

The overall quality and definition of the Sankey photographs have provided an invaluable legacy for railway historians and modellers of today, and it has been the author's aim to present a pictorial record of the varied activities of the Furness Railway Company as captured largely through the lens of a photographer who was not himself a railway enthusiast.

Negative numbers have been provided, wherever possible, with each of the Sankey illustrations, and requests for prints may be made via the Publisher, quoting this number.

1.
THE MAIN LINE FROM CARNFORTH TO BARROW

The Furness Railway was opened for mineral traffic on 3 June 1846, although the official opening did not take place until 24 August. It was built primarily to carry iron ore mined in the Lindal and Dalton areas and slate from the Earl of Burlington's quarries at Kirkby to the sea at Barrow for shipping.

The passenger services connected with a steamer service to Fleetwood via a branch line to Rampside and the then privately owned Piel Pier, which extended into the sea at Roa Island.

Extension of the railway northwards from Kirkby to Broughton was completed in 1848, and Whitehaven was eventually reached in 1866 with the purchase of the Whitehaven & Furness Junction Railway. In the opposite direction a line to Ulverston had been completed by 1854, and acquisition, in 1862, of the 1857-opened Ulverston & Lancaster Railway as far as Carnforth finally gave the Furness Railway a main line 74 miles long with connections to the routes of the London & North Western Railway (LNWR) at both ends. Also in 1862 the Coniston Railway, running between Broughton and Coniston village at the head of Coniston Lake, was annexed, and in 1867 a connection with the Midland Railway network into Yorkshire was established by the opening of the Furness and Midland joint line from Carnforth to Wennington.

Further expansion came with the opening, in 1869, of the Lakeside branch, a line built with tourist traffic very much in mind, followed by mineral branches to the quarry at Stainton, also in 1869, the iron ore mines at Stank in 1873 and a line to serve the newly opened North Lonsdale Iron Works in 1874. It was the intention to extend this line to the nearby village of Bardsea, thence to Barrow by means of a connection into the Stank branch near to Roose, but apart from some earthworks the extension never progressed beyond Conishead Priory, at that time a hydropathic hotel with its own golf course and served by an attractive little station, built in 1882, which still stands. At the same time a single-track branch between the London & North Western main line at Hincaster, just south of Oxenholme, and the Furness main line at Arnside was opened to facilitate the movement of coke from the Durham coalfield to the iron works at Ulverston, Barrow and Askam. This branch also enabled the Furness Railway to obtain running rights to operate passenger services as far as Kendal on the London & North Western Railway's Windermere branch.

During this time of expansion of the railway, the small port of Barrow grew from a hamlet of some 30 cottages in 1846 to a thriving industrial town of 16,000 inhabitants by the time its charter was granted in 1867. By the early 1880s the population had risen to 47,000, providing the workforce for a wide variety of industries, including shipbuilding, iron and steel production, and jute and paper manufacture, in addition to those employed by the Railway Company itself in its offices, docks, workshops and on operating the line.

Below Carnforth station became the southern terminus of the Furness Railway in 1862 when the Company acquired the Ulverston & Lancaster Railway, which had been opened in 1857. It was the Company's junction with the West Coast Main Line of the London & North Western Railway (LNWR), which can be seen on the right of the picture, the Furness Railway operating in and out of the single curving platform on the left. To overcome the operating restrictions

imposed by the single platform, a cross-over, just visible behind the boy messenger, was installed to allow two trains to use the platform at the same time.

Connection was also made here with the Midland Railway via the 1867-opened Wennington branch, a line jointly owned by both companies and which linked Carnforth with Wennington on the Midland-controlled 'Little North Western' line from Lancaster to Skipton. This gave the Furness Railway access to Yorkshire and conversely the Midland Railway an outlet into the Lake District. The platform for this branch is the bay visible in the left background, beyond the Furness platform, where Midland coaches can be seen.

The station as pictured here was opened on 2 August 1880, replacing an earlier LNWR and FR joint station and a Furness and Midland joint station. At the same time a curve was constructed to allow trains from Leeds to run directly into the new station. The fine overall roof was demolished in the late 1930s to allow construction of a second platform and buildings on the Furness side of the station which are still in use, but trains on the main line no longer call at Carnforth, as the platforms on the LNWR side were removed when the West Coast Main Line was electrified in the early 1970s.

Station foreman George Norman (no relation to the author) converses with a junior employee on the left. The fine station clock, made by Joyce of Whitchurch, a major clockmaker to the LNWR, was probably installed in 1880. *2065*

Opposite below Carnforth station wore a sad and neglected look when photographed in August 1999. Taken of necessity from a slightly different position, Edward Sankey's viewpoint being obscured by the screen on the right, the concrete awnings and Barrow-bound platform on the extreme left-hand side are a legacy of the 1938 rebuild by the London Midland & Scottish Railway Company (LMS).

The station clock retains its original position, albeit not the original clock but a later electric version of about 1970, which, as might be expected on a station in such a run-down state, is not in working order. The bookstall too has long since disappeared, as has the refreshment room, immortalised in the 1945 film *Brief Encounter*. The only visible survivors from the original scene are the truncated vertical roof supporting pillars and the subway guard rails.

Help is at hand, however, and the Carnforth Station and Railway Trust, in association with Railtrack, the station's owner, are in the midst of a renovation and revitalisation programme. When complete this will see the installation of small cottage industries in the station buildings, the restoration of the refreshment room and the refurbishment of the station clock with its original mechanism. *Author*

Above Silverdale, the first call after leaving Carnforth, is, like so many rural stations, some distance from the village it was built to serve and from which it takes its name. Originally on the Ulverston & Lancaster Railway (U&LR), the station building on the down, left-hand, platform is similar in design to that at Cark in Cartmel, comprising booking office, waiting room and Station Master's house. The signal box and waiting shelter on the up platform are typical of those to be seen on many small Furness Railway stations, although the shelter, still standing today but out of use, is built on a grander scale than those at many other small stations. Silverdale is now an unstaffed halt with a limited service, but the main building still exists and was for a few years a restaurant named 'Coppernob'. Recently extended, it has since been converted to private residences. *CRA, Pattinson Collection PA0017*

Above Arnside station, junction for the Hincaster branch, serves a small seaside resort, which until completion of the U&LR in 1857 was only a tiny fishing village of some 20 dwellings. From these small beginnings the village was developed by the Furness Railway into a thriving holiday resort.

This scene, looking along the up or Carnforth-bound platform, features the iron footbridge constructed in 1910 by the Clyde Structural Iron Co at a cost of £258, following letters of complaint from the local vicar. He was concerned about the danger to passengers having to cross the main line by means of a level crossing when travelling to Carnforth or using the branch line to Kendal, which operated from a platform on the left-hand side of the up platform. The original building on this joint platform was of timber construction in a mock-Tudor style, but this was replaced in 1914 by the present-day brick building, which is now the headquarters of the Arnside/Silverdale Area of Outstanding Natural Beauty Landscape Trust.

The down or Barrow-bound platform building, seen through the footbridge, is of Ulverston & Lancaster Railway design, similar to those at Silverdale and Cark. The latter two buildings still exist, but that at Arnside was demolished early in 1987, to be replaced by a simple waiting shelter. *5035*

Above right A Furness Railway 0-6-2 tank engine crosses the 522-yard-long screw pile viaduct over the River Kent at Arnside with an up mixed goods train. A dominant feature of the village, the viaduct was built by John Brunlees for the U&LR during 1856/7 as a single-track structure. It was widened to take double track in 1863 shortly after the Furness Company had taken over the line. Further

modifications were needed by 1885 when the original cast iron girders were replaced by wrought iron, the work being completed by 1887, and this picture, probably taken in 1914, shows the viaduct in that form. *5053*

Right By the beginning of the 20th century considerable deterioration was taking place in the cast iron columns of the Kent Viaduct between the water line and the river bed. As a result a 20mph speed limit was imposed with effect from 1 January 1913. Plans to build brick piers round the existing columns and increase the number of piers were formulated in August 1913, but refurbishment was temporarily postponed in order that the Leven viaduct, which was also in poor condition, could be renewed first.

Messrs Coulton Hunter of Barrow were the contractors responsible for the work on both viaducts, and the rebuilding at Arnside, which eventually commenced during May 1915, was completed in October 1917. During this rebuilding, heavy wartime traffic necessitated the opening of a special signal box at the west end of the viaduct with tablet machines to allow single-line working while building work was in progress. Further refurbishment of the piers and renewal of the decking commenced in 1990 and was continued each summer, when single-line working was introduced for periods of approximately six weeks at a time to allow engineers to progressively renew the Carnforth line decking and the timbers on which the rails are laid. The work is now complete.

In this post-1923 scene a goods train of 57 vehicles, including an ex-Furness Railway goods brake-van and two gunpowder vans, is crossing the viaduct on its way to Barrow. *9359*

THE FURNESS RAILWAY

THE MAIN LINE FROM CARNFORTH TO BARROW 11

Above The pleasant holiday resort of Grange-over-Sands owes its existence and prosperity, in its modern form, to the coming of the railway in 1857. Built shortly after the track was doubled in 1866, the present station buildings replaced an earlier U&LR structure similar to those at Cark and Silverdale. This exterior view of the station is little different from today. The ivy has been removed from the walls and there are rather more motor cars than the solitary vehicle, registration K 487, which is under scrutiny from the driver of the horse-drawn vehicle on the right. The station forecourt is now a car park and the trees on the right have given way to an underground pumping station and ornamental garden. *4144*

Above right This early view of Grange-over-Sands station was taken looking westwards from Blawith Rocks before the promenade was built (see below). On the right is a 2-2-2WT locomotive, dwarfed by the horse box it appears to be setting on or taking off a train of four-wheeled, brown-liveried coaching stock. The engine on the left, at the head of the train, is a 2-4-0 tender engine of a type supplied to the Furness Railway between 1870 and 1882 by Sharp Stewart for passenger train use. The arrival of the 2-4-0s meant that the 2-2-2WTs were relegated to branch-line and shunting duties, and while the number of the engine in this picture is not wholly clear, it seems to be No 37, which would date the scene as before 1897, as No 37 was converted to a stationary boiler in Barrow Works in that year. *Author's collection*

Right The promenade westwards from the station to Bayley Lane, where there was once a small pier, was built by the Furness Railway in about 1900. Extensions further west to Carter Lane and eastwards from the station subway to Blawith Rocks, where the railway was crossed by a still extant footbridge, were carried out during the period 1902-4, largely through the generosity of one Harold Porritt JP, a wealthy industrialist who had come to live in Grange in 1895.

This 1920s view of the station is again little changed today. The goods shed on the right still stands, but is not in railway use; it now houses a small local industry. *9511*

THE FURNESS RAILWAY

Below After the acquisition of the Ulverston & Lancaster line by the Furness Railway, it was the directors of the latter company, always on the look-out for ways to attract customers, who were responsible for the building, in 1886, of the attractive Grange Hotel at Grange-over-Sands. Standing on high ground overlooking the village, the hotel was designed in an Italianate style to complement the 'Swiss chalet' appearance of the nearby station buildings, seen here. In addition, the resort's attractive ornamental gardens and small lake were constructed in 1894 on reclaimed land, drained by the Furness Railway Company. The substantial station buildings, platforms and awnings have changed very little in the 80 or more years since this photograph was taken. *2804*

Above right Heading for Kents Bank, the line curves around the coast adjacent to the 1900-built promenade. Here an up passenger train, containing LNWR coaches and headed by a 4-4-0 locomotive, passes Grange's tall up distant signal, sited on the down side for better visibility, on its way to Grange station. In the background can be seen Clare House Pier, believed to have been built with timbers from the dismantled deep water pier at Roa Island. From here pleasure sailings around the bay were operated when the tide was suitable, and on occasions small steamers, sailing out of Morecambe, would call. The bandstand at the shoreward end of the pier was moved away from the railway in 1928 following complaints about noise and smoke spoiling the concerts, but the footbridge and refreshment kiosk behind it remain to this day. The outdoor swimming pool, opened in August 1932, now occupies the site of the pier, and a second pier, located at Bayley Lane, has also completely disappeared. *4142*

Right The delightful small hamlet of Kents Bank originated at the starting point of the route across the sands of Morecambe Bay to Hest Bank which, until the opening of the U&LR in 1857, had been the most important route between the Furness peninsular and the rest of Lancashire since monastic times. This view of Kents Bank station from the eastern end features a typical Furness Railway country station signal box with an 0-6-0 tender engine on the up or Carnforth-bound line having the all clear from the Up Starter, a lower-quadrant signal with a winch-operated lamp and, from its corrugated appearance, a metal arm. The signal box colosed on 26 June 1943. *5843*

THE FURNESS RAILWAY

THE MAIN LINE FROM CARNFORTH TO BARROW 15

Above Another view of Kents Bank station, looking towards Grange-over-Sands. The time is 2.10pm and an afternoon train, conveying a Midland Railway clerestory coach, is drawing in on its way to Barrow in the charge of an 0-6-0 tender locomotive. The frock-coated Station Master unfortunately obscures the buffer beam, making positive identification of the engine impossible, but this is one of a class of 19, designed by William Pettigrew, the Furness Railway Locomotive & Carriage Superintendent, which were introduced progressively between 1913 and 1920 for hauling heavy mineral trains. A number of these locomotives, after being fitted with steam-heating apparatus and the vacuum brake, were frequently to be seen on passenger trains on the Furness Railway main line.

The gabled stone building on the extreme left of the picture is the station house dating from U&LR days, and the stone and wooden extension containing waiting rooms and toilets was added by the Furness Railway in the 1890s. This photograph was taken before the platform widening, for which approval was given in October 1914, had been carried out. This wooden extension was removed when replacement became necessary during the 1950s, and the platform reverted to its original width. *2668*

Left The station that serves the adjoining villages of Cark and Flookburgh together with nearby Cartmel, known in Furness Railway days as Cark in Cartmel and nowadays as Cark and Cartmel, was also the home station of the Holker Hall residence of the Cavendish family, who figured so prominently in the early history of the Railway. It was the head of the family, the Duke of Devonshire, who was one of the principal champions of the Furness Railway Company in the pioneering days of the early 1840s and who became its Chairman in 1848.

WEEK DAYS. / SUNDAYS.

DOWN.

	1	2	3	4	5	6	7	8	9	10	11	12	13	14	15	16	17	18	19	20	21	22	23	24	1	2	3	4	5	6	7	8
CARNFORTH ....dep	4 25																															

(Timetable: MAIN LINE — DOWN, with station rows CARNFORTH, Silverdale, Arnside, Grange, Kents Bank, Cark and Cartmel, ULVERSTON, Lindal, Dalton, Furness Abbey, Roose, BARROW Central Stn., R'sden Dock; then BARROW, Askam, Kirkby, Foxfield, Green Road, Millom, Silecroft, Bootle, Eskmeals, Ravenglass, Drigg, Seascale, Sellafield, Braystones, Nethertown, St. Bees, WHITEHAVEN.)

** Horses and Private Carriages are not conveyed locally by these trains. ** Horses and Private Carriages are not conveyed by these trains. **A** Stops to set down Passengers on informing the Guard at the preceding stopping Station, and by signal when required to take up Passengers. **B** Till September 19th only. **C** Tuesdays, Thursdays and Saturdays only. **D** Stops to set down Passengers from Stations beyond Carnforth only on informing the Guard at Carnforth. **E** Daily until September 19th, and afterwards on Thursdays and Saturdays only. **F** Till September 19th stops by signal to take up Passengers for Ulverston, Haverthwaite, Lindal and Stations beyond only. **G** Stops to set down Passengers from Ulverston and Stations beyond only on informing the Guard at Ulverston. **H** A Carriage slipped. **J** Stops by signal to take up Passengers for Belfast only on Tuesdays, Thursdays, and Saturdays. **L** Via Dalton. † Runs beyond Silecroft commencing July 13th. ‡ 7 mts. earlier from Foxfield to Silecroft until July 11th.*

WEEK DAYS. / SUNDAYS.

UP.

	1	2	3	4	5	6	7	8	9	10	11	12	13	14	15	16	17	18	19	20	21	22	23	24	25	1	2	3	4	5	6	7
WHITEHAVEN Br'sty dep																																

(Timetable: MAIN LINE — UP, with station rows WHITEHAVEN, St. Bees, Nethertown, Braystones, Sellafield, Seascale, Drigg, Ravenglass, Eskmeals, Bootle, Silecroft, Millom, Green Road, Foxfield, Kirkby, Askam, BARROW Central Stn. & R'sden Dock; then BARROW, Roose, Furness Abbey, Dalton, Lindal, ULVERSTON, Cark and Cartmel, Kents Bank, Grange, Arnside, Silverdale, CARNFORTH.)

**** Horses and Private Carriages are not conveyed by this Train on Mondays. **A** Stops to set down Passengers on informing the Guard at the preceding stopping station, and by signal to take up Passengers. **C** Tuesdays, Thursdays and Saturdays only. **E** Daily until Sept. 19th, and afterwards on Thursdays and Saturdays only. **G** Stops to set down Passengers from Ulverston and stations beyond on informing the Guard at Ulverston. **L** Stops by signal to take up Passengers for stations beyond Carnforth only. **M** Stops by signal to take up Passengers for Ulverston or beyond on Thursdays only. **N** Stops by signal to take up Passengers for Skipton, Crewe and Stations beyond only. **P** Stops to set down passengers from Whitehaven on informing the Guard at Whitehaven. **Q** Stops to set down passengers from stations North of Barrow on informing the Guard at Barrow. † Till July 11th only. ‡ Commencing July 13th.*

A country station with down platform building and offices similar to those at Silverdale, the up platform facilities were much more substantial than the simple wooden waiting shelter normally provided at rural stations. Designed by Paley & Austin and probably built in the 1870s, it even boasted an awning. Could this have been a result of its use by the Cavendish family and the important, occasionally Royal, visitors to Holker Hall? There was also a goods shed (most stations had one), a cattle dock and a signal box, which was replaced by a larger LMS box in about 1953, and not closed until January 1998. An ornate cast iron footbridge was installed at some time after this photograph was taken.

The down platform building still stands, but in private ownership, while that on the up platform, having already lost its awning, was demolished in 1986, despite strenuous efforts by local railway groups for its preservation. It was replaced by a very unattractive little shelter built from concrete blocks and artificial stone. *W. Anderson collection*

Above Main-line trains from the 1914 Summer Timetable, pocket edition.

The time according to Ulverston station clock is 1.23pm, and the 1.00pm lunchtime express from Barrow, due to arrive in Ulverston at 1.18pm, is drawing away from No 2 platform 3 minutes late (see the lower half of column 9 in the lower timetable on the previous page).

The Furness Railway extension from Dalton (Crooklands) reached Ulverston, as a single track, in 1854 and ran into a wooden building, sited in what was later to become Ulverston goods yard, which was destroyed by the elements at the beginning of 1855. Doubling of the track was completed in 1858, by which time the more substantial station building, located beyond the railway on the right of the picture, had been built; the roof is just visible above the wall. For a time this was the terminus of the Furness Railway and passengers travelling onwards joined trains on the Ulverston & Lancaster Railway using a lower level station by means of steps located at the end of the railings seen above the locomotive. Designed by the Lancaster architects Paley & Austin, the station shown here is the third, opened in 1874, having been tendered for at £9,025 by its builders. It is today a listed building, as indeed is the 1858 structure, which was converted to a prestige motor car showroom during 1989. The station nameboard on the left informs passengers that Ulverston was the junction station for the Lakeside (Windermere) and Conishead branches.

The train is headed by 1913-introduced 4-4-0 passenger locomotive No 130. The express was scheduled to call only at Ulverston and Grange, although on request it would stop at Furness Abbey to set down passengers from stations north of Barrow and pick up those, presumably guests from Furness Abbey Hotel, travelling to stations beyond Carnforth, where there were connections with LNWR services to Glasgow and Edinburgh in the north and Liverpool, Manchester and London Euston in the south.

It is interesting to note that while the station dates from 1874, the clock in the tower was not installed until 1902 when the Company's Traffic & Works Committee, at its meeting on 22 April of that year, asked the General Manager to obtain tenders for striking and non-striking clocks with opal dials for night illumination and to submit these to the Deputy Chairman for consideration. In the event a striking clock was installed, made by Joyce of Whitchurch, who was also responsible for the clock at Carnforth station (see page 9). The striking gong was removed during the 1950s after complaints from nearby residents, and at some time after that the clock itself ceased to function. Several years of inactivity followed until Mr D. E. Burns, a clockmaker from Ulverston, restored it in April 1997, and now, wound up once a week by Mr Burns, it once again tells rail passengers and townspeople alike the correct time. *5816*

A view from the western end of Ulverston station with a Carnforth-bound train in the up platform and milk churns being man-handled across the down, Barrow-bound, line. The need for an extension of the railway beyond Ulverston was recognised as early as 1850, and when the Ulverston & Lancaster Railway was given the Royal Assent on 25 July 1851 there were celebrations in the town that included the ringing of church bells. Opened as a single line only for goods traffic on 10 August 1857 and for passengers on the 26th of the same month, trains on the new railway were worked by locomotives and rolling-stock on loan from the Furness Company. By 1860 the two systems had been integrated and in May 1862 the Furness Company purchased the U&LR, at the same time buying the Ulverston Canal. The island platform between the two lines was to allow easy interchange of passengers between main-line trains and those operating on the Lakeside branch. *5828*

Above The train in No 1 platform at Ulverston, on its way to Barrow, carries a through LNWR carriage from Manchester to Whitehaven, which can be seen on the right of the picture at the rear of the train. These through carriages were conveyed on one morning and one afternoon train, the morning carriage leaving Manchester Exchange at 10.15am, reaching Barrow at 1.11pm and Whitehaven at 2.53pm, while the afternoon service operated from Manchester Victoria, departing at 2.55pm, arriving in Barrow at 5.42pm and Whitehaven at 7.10pm. In the opposite direction the coaches left Whitehaven at 11.40am and 2.40pm, arriving in Manchester at 4.15pm and 7.30pm respectively.

The station refreshment room was situated on this platform and can be seen on the left of the picture. It survived until just after the Second World War and was demolished in around 1960, although its outline can still be seen on the platform. *5824*

Below No 73, a 2-4-2 tank engine ambles leisurely into the down platform at Ulverston with a train probably from Lakeside. Built as a 2-4-0 tender engine in 1872, No 73 was rebuilt as a tank engine in 1891 and scrapped in 1919.

Seats with the 'squirrel and grapes' ornamentation, unique to the Furness Railway and eagerly sought after by railwayana collectors of today, can be seen on the up platform, while on the goods avoiding line a 20mph speed restriction has been imposed.

'Squirrel and grapes' platform seats were to be seen at Ulverston station until 1979, and a number of these now grace local gardens (a restored end is seen here). Today only two seats of this pattern remain, to fulfil the requirements of the building's listed status. Kept in the booking hall, they are reproductions made from fibreglass. The origin of the design is not known, but one unsubstantiated and rather fanciful tale tells how Sir James Ramsden, having his breakfast at the Furness Abbey Hotel, saw a squirrel eating nuts on the lawn and it was this that gave him the idea. *5823*

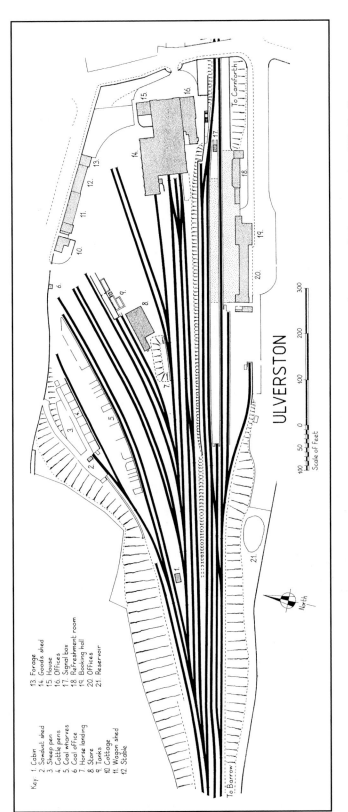

Key:
1. Cabin
2. Sawdust shed
3. Sheep pen
4. Cattle pens
5. Coal wharves
6. Coal office
7. Horse landing
8. Store
9. Tanks
10. Cottage
11. Wagon shed
12. Stable
13. Forage
14. Goods shed
15. House
16. Offices
17. Signal box
18. Refreshment room
19. Booking hall
20. Offices
21. Reservoir

ULVERSTON

100 50 0 50 100 200 300
Scale of Feet

To Barrow
To Carnforth

North

Above Map of Ulverston station. *Mike Faulkner*

Left A list of through carriages to and from the Furness Railway system from the Summer Timetable of 1914, as referred to opposite.

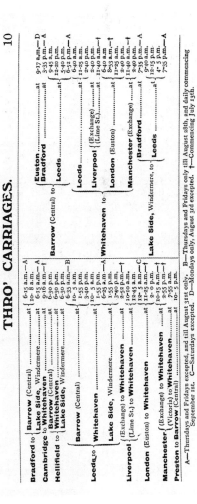

THRO' CARRIAGES.

10

Bradford to { Barrow (Central)	...at {	6·15 a.m.—A 10· 8 a.m.—A
Cambridge to Whitehaven	...at	9·16 a.m.—†
Hellifield to { Whitehaven	...at	6·30 p.m.
Lake Side, Windermere	...at	6·30 p.m.—B
Leeds to { Barrow (Central)	...at {	10· 5 a.m. 1·55 p.m. 3·40 p.m.
Whitehaven	...at	6·25 a.m.—A
Lake Side, Windermere	...at	1·55 p.m.
Liverpool { (Exchange) to Whitehaven	...at {	3·40 p.m. 2·40 p.m.—†
(Lime St.) to Whitehaven	...at	10·30 a.m.
London (Euston) to Whitehaven	...at	12· 5 a.m.—C
Manchester (Exchange) to Whitehaven	...at	2· 0 p.m.
Preston to Barrow (Central)	...at	10·15 a.m.—†

Barrow (Central) to { Euston	...at	9·17 a.m.—D
Bradford		3·35 p.m.—A 9·45 a.m. 12·20 p.m. 5·40 p.m.
Leeds	...at {	6·52 p.m.—A 6·40 a.m. 1·25 a.m. 2·40 p.m.
Whitehaven to { Liverpool { (Exchange) (Lime St.)	...at	11·40 a.m.—† 8·53 a.m.—†
London (Euston)	...at	6·40 a.m 11·25 a.m.
Manchester (Exchange)	...at	11·40 a.m.—A 2·40 p.m.
Bradford		7·35 p.m.—A
Leeds	...at {	9·40 a.m. 12·15 p.m. 4· 5 p.m.
Lake Side, Windermere, to Leeds	...at	7·35 p.m.—A

A—Thursdays and Fridays excepted, and till August 31st only.   B—Thursdays and Fridays only till August 28th, and daily commencing September 1st.   C—Saturdays excepted.   D—Mondays only, August 3rd excepted.   †—Commencing July 13th.

Left Such an important interchange station as Ulverston required a large staff to operate it, and here they are, 15 strong, posing with Station Master Mr E. G. Woolgar at the western end of the down platform. It is interesting to note the variety of headgear, which in addition to uniform caps includes cloth caps and a straw boater.

Mr Woolgar, who was born in May 1860, started working on the Furness Railway at Ulverston on 11 August 1873 as an office boy earning 6s 6d per week. By 1878, as a clerk, this had risen to 20 shillings (£1.00) per week, and on his appointment as Station Master in 1896 his salary was £90 per annum. Mr Woolgar remained in the post at Ulverston until his retirement on 1 August 1919, when he was earning £450 per annum, a sizeable salary in those far-off years, and it is possible that this photograph was taken to mark that occasion.

This end of the platform and the rooms behind are now occupied by a privately owned entertainment club appropriately named 'Buffers'. *5832*

Below left An evocative glimpse of the drawing-room in the Station Master's house at Ulverston, which the occupants would have certainly called 'the parlour'. Although not dated, the picture is undoubtedly pre-1914 and shows typical furnishings of the time, which a few decades ago would have been dismissed as 'Victorian clutter' but which nowadays would qualify as a display of desirable antiques. The walls, covered by heavily patterned wallpaper, are hung with a multitude of pictures, and photographs adorn the mantelpiece of the marble fireplace surround with its cast iron grate and tiled sides. Note the bellows on the right for blowing up a reluctant fire, the fender and fire irons in front, the ornate brackets of the gas lamps on each side of the chimney breast, with their round glass shades, the hearth rug, the brass candlestick on the

bookcase, and the antimacassar on the back of the armchair. Cluttered maybe, but with a friendly cosiness often missing from modern sitting-rooms. *5836*

Below A seven-coach passenger train bound for Barrow passes the western end of Lindal Ore Sidings behind 4-4-0 passenger locomotive No 133. Coming into service in 1914, this locomotive was the last of 20 of a class introduced between 1890 and 1914 by the Furness Railway, and had the distinction of carrying the highest number allocated by the Company to any of its locomotive stock. The 4-4-0s hauled main-line passenger trains, sometimes double-headed, until the appearance of the 4-6-4 'Baltic' tanks in 1920.

At the time that this photograph was taken, the ore sidings would have been thronged with wagons filled with iron ore hewn from the many mines in the Lindal area, and in the background can be seen the buildings and chimneys of Lowfield Pit. It was close to this spot, in the sidings on the right of the picture, that Sharp Stewart 0-6-0 goods engine No 115 was engulfed in a huge crater, caused by subsidence, while shunting on 22 September 1892. Driver Postlethwaite and Fireman Robinson jumped to safety and the tender was saved, but the locomotive disappeared and is now thought to be some 200 feet beneath the surface, possibly in old mine workings that honeycomb the earth in this area. From time to time various schemes have been proposed to locate, and if possible recover, the old engine, but to date no attempt has been made.

The locomotive number of the lost engine was not used again until 1898, when sister locomotive 114 was allocated the vacant number to allow 114 to be given to one of the new 0-6-2 tank locomotives being introduced at that time. In 1920 the number 115 was re-allocated once again to the first of the five new 'Baltic' tanks, the 0-6-0 being renumbered 70. *5849*

Lindal station, with its two platforms and goods avoiding line seen on the right of the picture, opened when the Furness Railway extension to Ulverston reached Lindal in 1851, and closed to passengers just 100 years later in 1951. The sandstone waiting shelter on the up (right-hand) platform was built in 1898 at a cost of £90 following representations from Dalton-in-Furness Urban District Council. The provision of the footbridge, again requested by Dalton UDC, was raised several times before it was finally erected in 1908. It remained at Lindal until the station closed, after which it was dismantled and re-erected at Kirkby where it can still be seen. The goods shed, signal box and sidings are just visible beyond the footbridge, while in the background on the left are the buildings of Lindal Cote mine. Also in the background, on the right, smoke and steam can be seen issuing from the eastern portal of Lindal Tunnel, which at 440 yards was one of only four tunnels on the Furness Railway main line.

Both these views were taken from the road bridge at the eastern end of the station looking towards Barrow, and in the earlier one 0-6-2 tank engine No 108 can be seen entering the station at the head of an up passenger train. Built by the North British Locomotive Company, No 108 entered service in 1907 and carried a number previously allocated to a tank engine named *Wastwater*, which had been acquired in 1878 when the Whitehaven, Cleator & Egremont Railway passed into the joint ownership of the Furness and LNWR companies. Becoming LMS No 11637 in 1923, the engine was scrapped in 1935.

As seen in the second view, today there is no trace of the station's existence, although the retaining wall on the right of the avoiding line is still to be seen. *2546/Author*

Above Dalton was the terminus for passenger services when they were first introduced by the Furness Railway in August 1846, although the line extended for several hundred yards beyond the station to Crooklands, where iron ore, mined nearby, was collected for transportation to the shipping jetties on the coast at Barrow. The wooden goods shed on the left of this 1930s picture occupies the site of the original station. The illustrated station was built in about 1870, at the same time that Station Road, which at the time crossed the railway on the level, was raised to cross by the overbridge just visible at the far end of the right-hand platform. The station then had, and indeed still has, up and down main-line platforms, but an up (left-hand-side) bay, a down loop and a substantial goods yard are now gone. The platform awning on the down side, which was originally of wooden construction, was rebuilt with iron supports in 1915. The main station building, the gabled roof of which can be seen on the left, still exists, but like so many other small station buildings is now a private residence. The awnings on both platforms were taken down in 1976, leaving the now unmanned station a rather desolate place. The station signal box, seen through the overbridge, closed on 12 October 1966. *CRA, Pattinson Collection PA0082*

Above right The up platform building and integral signal box of Furness Abbey station, opened in 1847, date from the mid-1860s. For some time after the opening of the U&LR in 1857 the station was the interchange point on the route north from Carnforth to Whitehaven, trains entering from Carnforth and reversing out again after portions for Barrow and Piel had been detached. A curve between Dalton and

Thwaite Flat, built in 1858, provided a direct route north, but it was not until 1873 that the interchange was transferred from Furness Abbey to Dalton. At that time also there was a bay beyond the up platform that served Coniston trains.

Even after the removal of the interchange, Furness Abbey continued to be a station of importance serving the Company's prestigious Furness Abbey Hotel (see Volume 2), the covered approach to which is the lower roof at the near end of the up platform. This was also the subway to the down platform, which in the era of this picture was an island. The platform levels were raised to 2ft 9in above rail level in September 1906 to make them the same as those at Barrow Central station. The down loop was removed in around 1936, and the up platform waiting shelter was demolished, not, like so many other country stations, under the axe of Dr Beeching, but many years earlier by a German land-mine during the air raids of 3-4 May 1941. Passenger services were finally withdrawn from Furness Abbey on 25 September 1950. *133*

Below The down island platform at Furness Abbey, with its through loop, can clearly be seen in this photograph, together with the bay on the right, which housed the private saloon of Sir James Ramsden, General Manager and later Managing Director of the Furness Railway until his retirement in 1895. Sir James lived in a railway-owned mansion, Abbots Wood, built close to the station in 1851.

Note the ground frame on the right-hand side of the picture, brought into use on 11 July 1892 to control movements on that side of the station. Also of interest is the arm on the Stevens-manufactured Up Home signal post with its distinctive ball-and-spike finial. The down platform building, signal box and up waiting room, all of which survived the bombing of May 1941, were not demolished until 1952. *3947*

Bottom Roose station, seen here in the late 1930s looking towards Barrow, is on the original Furness Railway line. It was at Roose Junction (sometimes referred to as Rampside Junction), just beyond the road bridge, that the 1846 line diverged, one branch going to the passenger steamer landing stage at Roa Island and the other to the iron ore jetties on the coast at Barrow. The junction closed in 1882 when steamer services were transferred to the newly opened Ramsden Dock station and landing stage. Note the low-level signal repeater arms beyond the bridge, so placed because the parapet obscured the high-level arms from the view of train crews while standing in the station. The bridge, carrying the road to Roose village and beyond, was authorised in 1866 to replace three original level crossings at a time when the Company was seeking to reduce the large numbers of level crossings over its line, which were causing serious disruption to services, by building overbridges.

In this track-level view, the trailing point on the left led to a short siding serving Yarlside mine, which remained in production until the 1940s. The station had a small signal box (closed on 26 January 1965) and a coal yard, and was under the jurisdiction of the station master at Furness Abbey, who at the time of this photograph was Mr R. A. Brunskill. Roose is now an unstaffed halt with a bus-type shelter on the up (right-hand) platform. *CRA, Pattinson Collection PA0088*

2.
BARROW-IN-FURNESS

Right The approach road to Barrow Central station with its gates (closed on one day each year to maintain private road status) was photographed on a snowy morning in November 1915. The notices on the hoardings on the right advertise excursions to Blackpool (by train, as the cross-bay steamers had been terminated because of the war), Ravenglass, for the newly opened narrow-gauge railway to Eskdale, and Whitehaven. The approach road left Abbey Road at its junction with Holker Street and Rawlinson Street, making an awkward five-road intersection, which, even with the introduction of traffic lights in the 1930s, became more and more hazardous as the volume of motor traffic increased. In recent times the junction has been simplified by moving the station approach entrance into Holker Street. For a number of years following the wartime bombing the station bookstall, previously sited on No 1 platform, was moved to occupy a site just beyond the gate on the left and remained there until the entrance was moved into Holker Street. The area to the left of the picture, which used to hold two carriage storage sidings known as 'Duke sidings' (named after the nearby Duke of Edinburgh Hotel), is, apart from a short stub behind the present station's car park, now occupied by a Ford motor car dealership. *3795*

Above right In this closer view of the station from the approach, 0-4-0 locomotive No 3, preserved and put on display in about 1902, can be seen in its glass case (see Volume 2). 'Coppernob', as it is known, is now part of the National Collection. In those traffic-free times children could play on the road in front of the station without fear of injury from the horse-drawn cabs waiting for passengers. But even in those early days a simple form of traffic control was being imposed, with incoming cabs being diverted to the left of the lamp standards. The wooden archway in the railings on the extreme right of the picture led to the excursion booking office, which had a roof to match that of the glass case housing 'Coppernob'; the vehicle shelter over the station entrance was erected in 1898 at a cost of £386. *95*

Above An armed soldier with fixed bayonet, wearing his Great War campaign medals, stands guard at the entrance to Barrow Central station during the railway strike of 1919. In addition to a board behind him drawing attention to a provisional train service from Friday 3 October 1919, there are other interesting posters. On the left the promenade at Grange-over-Sands is the subject, while at the Lakeside station refreshment pavilion hot and cold lunches are advertised as being served daily from 12.00 to 2.30pm, cost 2s 6d, and afternoon teas served between 4.00 and 6.00pm, at 1 shilling per head. Notice is also given of 'A New Express Train' running on Mondays and Saturdays only, departing from Barrow at 8.20 and calling at Ulverston and Grange, arriving in Carnforth at 9.30, where connections to Carlisle, Manchester and London Euston could be made. It is interesting to compare this service with a recent timetable that lists a diesel train leaving Barrow at 8.15, calling at all stations and arriving in Carnforth at 9.07, a saving of 18 minutes over the express timings of 1919, proving that services have improved during the last 74 years. *7511*

Below A sun-dappled view of the booking hall shows the ornate roof and decorative frieze in the brickwork. The picture can be dated by the notices on the right, one of which advertises the introduction of a new service to the Midland and North Eastern lines in 1920, while on the extreme left a poster draws attention to a rugby football match between Leigh and Barrow to be played at Little Park, Roose, on Saturday 12 February 1921, kicking off at 3.00pm. There are separate windows for 1st and 3rd Class passengers, and it can be seen that illumination by electric light has been introduced by this time. *7375*

Above In the days when railway tickets were punched and collected at stations instead of on trains as they are today, a Furness Railway Inspector poses proudly at the ticket barrier on No 1 platform of Barrow Central station. Beyond the sliding gates is a glimpse of the booking hall, while a poster advertising the opening of the new refreshment room at Seascale (see page 61) dates this picture as being taken in 1913, the construction of the Seascale refreshment room having been authorised by the Company's Traffic & Works Committee at its meeting on 27 May of that year. The function of this Committee, which met monthly, usually in Barrow, was to deal with matters directly concerning the running of the railway, while decisions regarding policy and capital expenditure were dealt with by the Board of Directors who met usually in London. *3919*

Below The interior of the left luggage office on platform 1 of Central station shows typical baggage of the day – Gladstone bags, wicker baskets and portmanteaus have been deposited, together with a quartet of bicycles. The porter in charge stares wide-eyed as he tries to keep still during the time exposure that would have been required to take this interior photograph on the relatively slow photographic plates of that time. *3923*

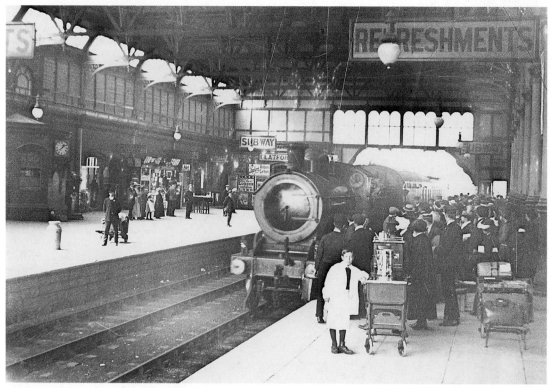

THE FURNESS RAILWAY

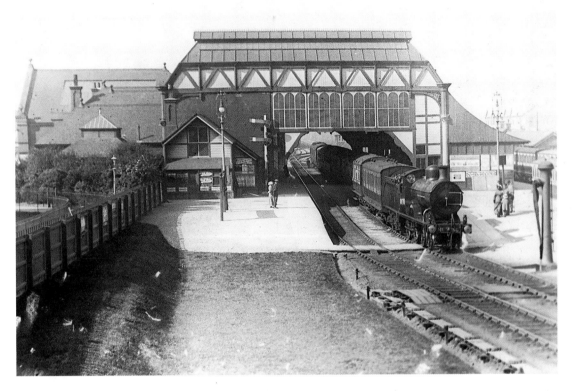

Above left Barrow Central station, opened on 1 June 1882, was the third station to serve passengers to and from Barrow. The first, a wooden platform at the quaintly named Rabbit Point, not far from the site of the present St George's church, was opened in 1846, to be followed in 1862 by a larger brick-built station in St George's Square (see page 38). This remained in use until a loop line, from Salthouse Junction to Thwaite Flat Junction, was installed, which, passing close to the centre of the town, offered a more suitable location for Barrow's main passenger station. At the time of opening, the buildings on No 1 platform were of a temporary nature, the offices, waiting and refreshment rooms seen to the left of this picture not being built until 1898, at which time the decision was taken to install electric light in the refreshment rooms, waiting rooms and offices on both platforms. The time on the station clock is 12.50, and passengers are gathering with their luggage, together with several milk churns, to await the arrival of the lunchtime Carnforth to Whitehaven express. *3689*

Left This picture was taken from the same viewpoint but 20 minutes later, at 1.10pm, and shows 4-4-0 passenger locomotive No 133 arriving, on time, with the 11.40am express from Whitehaven. An interesting footnote on the timetable states that this train did not convey horses and private carriages. Leaving Barrow at 1.15pm and calling only at Ulverston and Grange, it was timed to arrive at

Carnforth at 2.12pm. All eyes are on the incoming train except for those of the youthful refreshment trolley attendant who has obviously seen this event many times and is much more interested in the camera. *3688*

Above Another express train from the north, headed by 4-4-0 passenger engine No 130, built in 1913, stands in platform 2 at Barrow Central station, in a picture that shows to good advantage the fine mock-Tudor facade and overall roof.

The opening of the station in 1882 took place, according to a report in the *Barrow Times* of Saturday 3 June, without formality, and merited only a single paragraph, inserted in a column with the general heading 'Passing Notes'. The report does, however, record a more than passing interest in the new station by the townsfolk of Barrow, stating that 'during the day a large number of persons inspected the station and altogether Abbey Road presented an appearance of animation hitherto unknown to this locality.'

The first train from the south to arrive at the new station was the 4.40am from Carnforth, due to arrive at 5.40am, which, according to the newspaper, arrived a few minutes late, carrying a number of excursionists from Manchester. This train then continued to Whitehaven, timed to leave at 5.45am, while the first train south, which only ran as far as Ulverston, departed at 6.00am, arriving at its destination at 6.28am. The *Barrow Times* reported this train as carrying a large crowd of passengers 'in search of business and pleasure at the hiring fair at that town'. *3701*

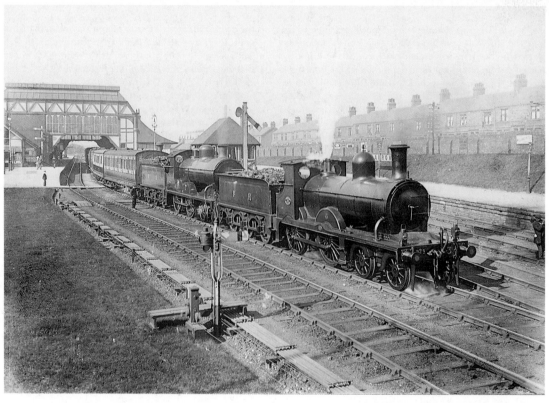

Left A 4-6-4 tank engine, probably No 119, accelerates away from Central station with a Carnforth-bound passenger train, the first three coaches of which appear to be LNWR vehicles, while in the loop through No 3 platform a goods train, headed by an 0-6-0 mineral engine, its number unfortunately obscured by the hose-pipe used to wash down the footplate, waits for the passenger to clear the main line before proceeding. Compare the length of the left-hand platform with the previous view – the extension took place in 1915, the platform being lengthened by 125 feet, while at the same time the up (right-hand) platform was extended by 71 feet to allow engines to take water without having to uncouple from their trains and run forward to the water column. *7390*

Below left A lunchtime express bound for Carnforth, conveying through coaches for London Euston, is about to leave No 2 platform in the charge of two immaculately groomed 4-4-0 passenger locomotives in about 1915. The pilot, No 33, is one of a batch of six such engines that first entered service in 1896, while the train engine is a later and more powerful locomotive, introduced in 1913, one of four tendered for at £3,670 each, although Mr Aslett secured a £20 reduction on each of the first two. No 130 became No 10185 at the Grouping in 1923 when the Furness Railway was absorbed by the LMS, and was scrapped in 1933.

An interesting signal that permitted movement in the up direction from the down, No 1, platform can be seen in the foreground. Built from sections of rail, the short signal post has a distinctly home-made appearance, and was in fact manufactured in the blacksmiths' shop of the Furness Railway workshops. The ground signal to the left of the post was made by Stevens & Sons of London. *3702*

Top The scene of devastation after the German Luftwaffe had dropped three land mines close to Barrow Central station on the night of 8th-9th May 1941. The presence of wagons in No 1 platform suggests that the enormous task of repairing the damage had already begun. *Dock Museum collection*

Middle The clearing-up operation after the bombing left Barrow station in a very spartan condition, as can be seen

in this picture taken from the road bridge at the southern end. Note the plinth on which 'Coppernob' had rested for nearly 40 years. *Author's collection*

Bottom Some 16 years after it had suffered at the hands of the German Air Force, Barrow station was rebuilt, and in 1957 British Railways unveiled this less than imposing structure. The only features of the old station to survive both bombing and reconstruction are the subway connecting the main-line platforms and the memorial, erected by the Furness Railway Company, to those employees who gave their lives during the Great War of 1914-18, which, still bearing the scars inflicted in 1941, has been re-erected in the booking hall. *A550*

Above In addition to the two covered platforms, Barrow Central had a through loop on the down side, served by platform 3, and there was also an up bay at the southern end of No 2 platform used by trains running on the Piel branch. Platform 4, shown here, came into use on 5 May 1907, costing £3,640 to build with its subway access, waiting shelter and gents toilet. However, this picture was taken many years later, in 1938, when a football special was about to leave Barrow for Wembley, carrying supporters of Barrow Rugby League Football Club to watch their team, which had reached the final of the Rugby League Challenge Trophy for the first time. Unfortunately Barrow fell at the last hurdle, losing the match to Salford. Surprisingly for an excursion train, the carriage stock is of late manufacture, the left-hand vehicle being a post-1934 Stanier design. *TP 180*

Below A detachment of the troops used to guard the various railway premises in Barrow during the railway strike of 1919 parades for the camera at the southern end of Central station. Behind the troops are the No 1 platform signals, home and distant arms on a common post with winch-operated lamps. On platform 2 shadowy figures can be seen, and one wonders if these are striking railwaymen or volunteers waiting to load the large number of milk kits on to a train.

The interesting enamel signs advertise a wide range of commodities including Wood Milne Rubber Heels, Brand's Essence of Beef, Veno's Cough Cure, Mazawattee Tea and Onoto, The Pen That Fills Itself. On the end wall of platform 2 beneath the Lifebuoy Soap advertisement is the well-known jingle 'They Came as a Boon and a Blessing to Men, The Pickwick, the Owl and the Waverley Pen'. *7512*

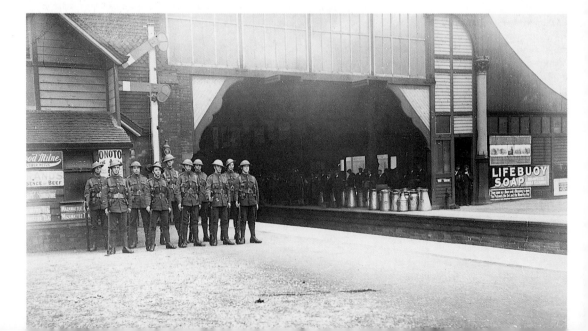

Above We now move towards the dockland area of Barrow Island (see the map overleaf). Shipyard station, one of two stations on the island, the other being at Ramsden Dock, was opened on 1 May 1899. Built at the request of Vickers Sons & Maxim to bring in workmen, who came from as far afield as Millom in the north and Grange-over-Sands in the south (there was also a service from Coniston), it originally consisted of a single platform, erected at a cost of £550, on an existing goods line serving the works through exchange sidings in what was later to become Bridge Road. Never intended for general public use, it served more than 1,700 workers daily in 1901. The second platform and crossover were installed in 1915, at which time the signal box,

fitted with block instruments, was opened to replace an original ground frame. The left-hand platform was used by the Grange train and the Millom train operated from that on the right. This picture and the one below can probably be dated in the early 1920s – an early motor car is visible crossing the tracks on its way from Anchor Road to Dunbar Street. This crossing was at one time controlled by a cross-bar signal. *A323*

Below The railings and gates, previously seen closed but here open, were erected at a cost of £100 in 1915, by which

time the station was in limited use for the general public. Sunday school trips were run, together with excursions to Rampside and Roa Island during the summer months, while during the winter special trains took supporters of Barrow Rugby League Football Club to Roose station in the days when the Club's headquarters were at Little Park there. The structure partially visible in the left foreground was an old coach body, converted for use as a booking office for the excursion trains. Services for workmen continued to operate until the closure of Buccleuch Dock bridge on 31 December 1966 forced their termination. *A320*

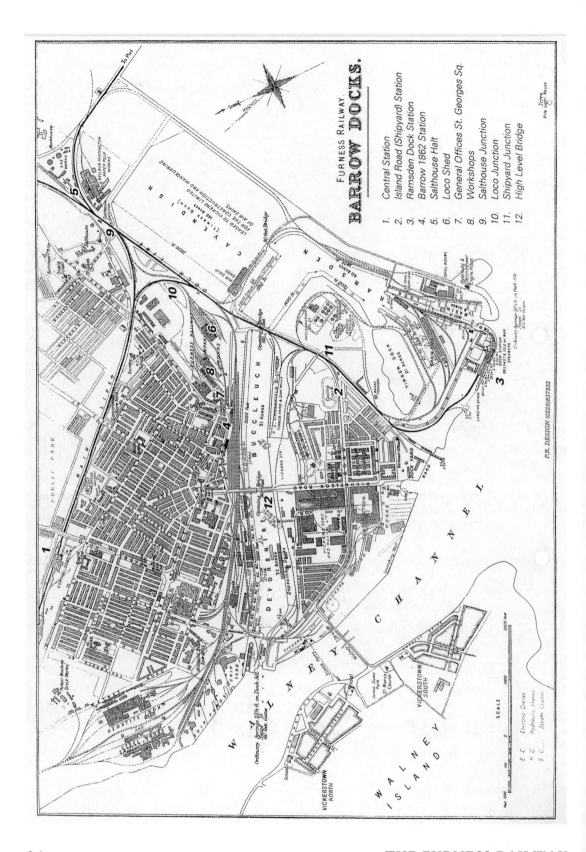

FURNESS RAILWAY.

BARROW DOCKS.

1. Central Station
2. Island Road (Shipyard) Station
3. Ramsden Dock Station
4. Barrow 1862 Station
5. Salthouse Halt
6. Loco Shed
7. General Offices St. Georges Sq.
8. Workshops
9. Salthouse Junction
10. Loco Junction
11. Shipyard Junction
12. High Level Bridge

P.R. DESIGN (0229)837933

Above The other station on Barrow Island, at Ramsden Dock, can be seen here beyond the Barrow Steam Navigation Company's screw steamer *Duchess of Devonshire*, which operated a service to the Isle of Man during the summer months and sailed between Barrow and Belfast in the winter. Opened on 1 June 1881, Ramsden Dock passenger station was built to deal with the boat train traffic transferred from Piel Pier when the deep-water berth was constructed in Walney Channel. Subsequently the station was extensively used in connection with the Railway Company's Lakeland Tours and it was here that holidaymakers from the Fylde, after crossing Morecambe Bay by paddle-steamer, transferred to the train to continue their tour (see Volume 2). This traffic ceased at the outbreak of the Great War in September 1914 and never really resumed, although an unsuccessful attempt was made to revive it in the late summer of 1922, using the screw steamer *Robina*, chartered from its owners W. A. & P. Cordingley. Used only occasionally thereafter for excursions, Ramsden Dock station was finally closed and pulled down in 1936. *299*

Below At the time of the opening of the Furness Railway in 1846 the General Offices of the Company were housed in the westernmost of the railway-built cottages in Salthouse Road. The building of new, more commodious premises began in the early 1850s on a site excavated into the south-western slopes of Rabbit Hill, adjacent to the early station, and by 1855 the southern portion of the building, together with the clock tower, had been erected. Completion was not until 1864, a date commemorated on a carved lintel surmounting a mullioned upper floor window that fortunately has survived, although not visible in this photograph.

The office building continued in use until 1966 and fulfilled a number of different roles during the many rationalisation exercises carried out after the nationalisation of Britain's railways in 1948. It was the Divisional Office when the Barrow Division was created in 1958, later becoming the headquarters of the Divisional Manager when the Barrow and Carlisle Divisions merged in 1964. By 1966, however, further restructuring saw the Barrow Division joining with Preston, and after 120 years railway management left Barrow. The offices finally closed in March 1966 with partial demolition following ten years later, in March 1976, in connection with a Council scheme to strengthen the retaining wall for nearby Salthouse Road. Complete demolition followed in August 1978, when the courts of Barrow Squash Club were built on the site. *60*

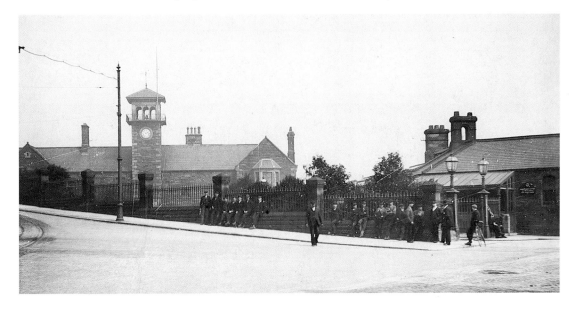

Above The view from the clock tower of the General Offices across St George's Square shows the 1862 station building with the bricked-up portals of the former train shed just visible on the left of the building. By 1872 this station, known after 1881 as Barrow Town, was becoming inadequate and was enlarged by the provision nearby of arrival platforms. Both parts closed when Barrow Central station opened on 1 June 1882, but both are still standing. The illustrated structure, now a Grade 2 listed building, is virtually unchanged, although for many years it has had no association with the working railway apart from a railwaymen's club being housed in one part of it. The converted carriage shed, after being used as a drill hall for the local Territorial Army unit, an Exhibition centre, a skating rink, a dance hall and a ten pin bowling alley, is now, in a greatly altered form, the home of the social club of a local factory. The picture can be dated by the vessel beneath the Vickers crane in Buccleuch Dock. This is the Clyde-built Cunard liner *Caronia*, which came to Barrow in 1924 for a complete refit. *A192*

Below Troops guard the General Offices in 1919, the posts of the entrance gates in St George's Square surmounted by two impressive lanterns. The carved window lintel commemorating the completion of the building in 1864 was located in the gable behind the left-hand gate-post. The tall chimney visible above the roof provided draught for the furnaces of the railway workshops and was sited in the middle of the junction of Salthouse Road and Rawlinson Street, in a part of Salthouse Road known to Barrovians as Big Chimney Hill. The chimney was taken down brick by brick during the 1930s after closure of the works. Today only that portion of offices on the extreme right of the picture exists and is recognisable. *7508*

During the Great War the amount of traffic using the Furness Railway system grew considerably. Steel production in the area was increased by the opening of new furnaces at Barrow and in West Cumberland; the amount of locally mined and imported ore rose from 198,000 tons in 1914 to 534,000 tons in 1917; imported oil, another valuable traffic, totalled about 180,000 tons passing through the docks; and munitions of all sorts were produced in the Vickers Works, the manufacture of which required a large traffic in workmen's trains, amounting to more than 300 train miles per day, to bring in the workers from outlying areas. All of this traffic had to be co-ordinated. The Furness Railway Company had for some time been considering the introduction of a train control system, and as the war progressed the need became imperative in order to meet these abnormal operating conditions. As a result a system was installed by the Company's electrical department and came into use on 1 February 1918. Operated by three controllers under a chief controller, the system was accommodated in the old passenger station buildings in St George's Square.

The control board covered the full 74-mile length of the main line, major sidings, and all lines in the Barrow area. It occupied the whole of one wall of the office and the Barrow controllers were in direct contact with their LNWR counterparts at Carnforth and Workington to facilitate movements in which both companies were involved. The photograph shows that section of the control board from Seascale in the north (left-hand end) to Grange-over-Sands in the south, with the Barrow area easily recognisable to the left of the rectangular reference panel. *7144*

FURNESS RAILWAY.

TRAIN CONTROL.

INSTRUCTIONS FOR THE CONTROL OFFICE STAFF.

(1) The Control Office will be open continuously, day and night, Weekdays and Sundays.

(2) The Controllers will be under the supervision of the Out-door Assistant to the Superintendent of the Line who will also act as Chief Controller, and their normal hours of duty will be as follows :—

> **1st Turn— 6-30 am. to 1-30 pm.**
> **2nd Turn— 1-30 pm. to 9-30 pm.**
> **3rd Turn— 9-30 pm. to 6-30 am.**

The three turns of duty will be worked round each week, and each man must book on 15 minutes before actually taking up duty, so that he may ascertain the position of affairs.

All turns of duty to be rostered and not altered without the concurrence of the Chief Controller.

(3) The principal duties of the Controllers will be :—

(a) To move the traffic from point to point as expeditiously as possible at the times required by the forwarding and receiving points, and to record on forms provided for the purpose particulars of the traffic to be moved.

(b) To obtain the maximum amount of work out of the Locomotive power supplied, by :—

> Using the fewest Locomotives possible.
> Incurring the minimum of light mileage.
> Securing the maximum workable loads.
> Preventing congestion and standing time by regulating converging streams of traffic.

Below A view of the marshalling yard taken from the tower of St George's church in about 1907. On the far side of Buccleuch Dock the Vickers fitting-out wharf is under construction, and the base of the tall crane, which is the viewpoint for the illustrations opposite, can just be seen behind the barges on the left.

Prominent in the middle distance is the original High Level Bridge, which carried road traffic across the railway and docks to Barrow Island, while the foreground shows a wealth of railway interest. Beyond the chimneypots on the right, with a semi-circular window in its gable end, is the roof of the 1872-built arrival platforms for the station in St George's Square (see page 38). In the marshalling yard itself is a line of empty North Eastern Railway coke wagons, awaiting return to the coke ovens of the Durham coalfield, and close to the white chimneys of the Barrow Harbour Hotel in the left foreground is a five-compartment, six-wheeled passenger coach. This type of carriage, often used on workmen's trains, seated 50 passengers, and more than 60 were built during the 1890s. *605*

Opposite above Barrow marshalling yard is now seen from the jib of the 150-ton hammerhead crane on the Vickers fitting-out wharf on the opposite side of Buccleuch Dock. The yard developed from sidings laid down on ground reclaimed during the 1850s on the west side of the Strand (this is the area behind the yard to the right of the high-level roadway). In 1859 a railway line from the sidings was laid down to serve the iron works of Schneider & Hannay, which was extended to Hawcoat Quarry in 1862 for transportation of sandstone to be used in the construction

of the dock walls. Buccleuch Dock opened in 1873, and it is from this period that the marshalling yard, seen here, can be dated.

In this very busy scene wagons can be identified from the Midland, LNWR, North British and Caledonian railways in addition to those of the Furness Railway. There are also a number of private owner wagons, prominent among which are several from the Featherstone Colliery in Yorkshire, suppliers of coal to the Vickers works.

This scene would be very different if photographed today; many of the buildings have now gone and in the region beyond the high-level Michaelson Road only the 1887-opened Town Hall would be seen. The remainder of this area is now dominated by Craven House, a large office block erected by Vickers in the 1960s. The marshalling yard closed on 1 September 1970 and the last remaining single track, which carried only limited trip traffic at the end, was lifted in 1989. Even the viewpoint would be different, as the crane from which this scene was photographed, erected in 1907, was toppled by a German bomb during the air raids of 1941 with the loss of two Vickers civil defence personnel, whose deaths are commemorated by a plaque fixed to the base of the replacement crane. *3932*

Opposite below This companion view, also taken from one of Vickers's tall hammer-head cranes, shows part of the goods yard further to the left, seen across Devonshire Dock. The goods yard was on the eastern side of the dock while the western side was occupied by the shipyard's fitting-out berths. At the time of construction – the Act empowering the Furness Railway Company to build

docks was obtained in 1863 and Devonshire Dock was opened officially on 19 September 1867 – the dock entrance was at the northern (left) end, through an entrance basin, but the building of Ramsden Dock, opened on 24 March 1879, allowed an entry to be made from the southern end of the system, and the northern access was closed. The fourth and largest of Barrow's docks, Cavendish Dock, was also completed in 1879, but never came into commercial use, being relegated to the role of a water feeder for the other three. Wagons bearing the names of the Lancashire & Yorkshire, Great Western, Great Central, Midland and Furness companies can be seen, but the presence of one or two LMS wagons dates the picture as post-1923.

Very few of the buildings beyond the yard now remain, apart from the steeply roofed chapel on the right, which, after serving for many years as a fruit and vegetable distribution warehouse, is now an entertainment club, and the Crown Printing Works, until 1991 the headquarters of the 1867-established Barrow Printing Company. The northern end of the dock was filled in during 1987 to permit the construction of a submarine building hall and ship-lift by Vickers, while the entrance basin is now a car park for the Dock Museum. A92

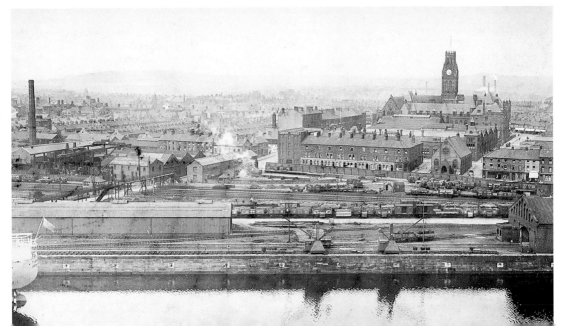

Above This view of Barrow goods yard was photographed from Michaelson Road at a point where it crossed the railway and the waterway between Devonshire and Buccleuch Docks on a high level bridge. In this bustling scene Fairbairn 0-4-0 locomotive No 14, one of four similar engines delivered in the period 1858-61, is taking water in the midst of some complicated pointwork, and to the right are two rebuilt Sharp Stewart 0-6-0 goods engines. In the background are the buildings of the Walmsley & Smith corn mill, and on the right Waddingtons foundry, with the footbridge known as Cornmill Crossing, from which the upper picture opposite was taken, just visible between the two. No 14 was scrapped in 1901 and the two 'Sharpies' rebuilt in 1898, so the picture can be quite closely dated. *Late G. Taylor collection*

Left As with many present-day pictures of railway locations, the scene has changed so dramatically that identification points for comparison purposes are not easy to find, and this August 1999 photograph of Barrow goods yard is no exception. It shows a desolate wasteland where once was busy railway activity; the coal depot on the right of the early picture is in the area of the curving security fence; Cornmill Crossing was sited at the brick building in the middle distance, which in the older view carries the Waddington nameboard; and the BAE Systems Devonshire Dock Shipbuilding Hall with its ancillary buildings roughly occupies the position of the old corn mill. *Author*

THE FURNESS RAILWAY

Above Another view of the northern end of the goods yard, looking north-east from the Cornmill Crossing footbridge. The through tracks in the centre served Barrow Steelworks and Vickers exchange sidings, and beyond Waddington's foundry on the right were Barrow cart sidings. All of this has now gone with the exception of the three-bay goods warehouse in the middle distance, which still stands and is easily recognisable although now partially hidden from this side by the giant submarine build hall of BAE Systems. The cart sidings site now carries a Tesco supermarket as part of a shopping precinct that occupies most of the land on the right of the picture. *59*

Above right Now the goods yard is seen looking south, from the other side of the cornmill on the extreme left of the previous photograph; part of the Cornmill Crossing overbridge can be seen in the background. The cornmill of Walmsley & Smith was opened as Barrow Steam Cornmill in 1871; sited on the eastern side of Devonshire Dock, it unloaded grain directly from the holds of ships tied up alongside into the storage silos on the right. Damaged during the air raids of May 1941, the mill finally closed in 1967 and the right-hand building and storage tanks were demolished soon afterwards. The building on the left survived as a fruit warehouse until December 1972 when it was gutted by fire, making immediate demolition necessary. The site is now incorporated into the BAE Systems submarine building complex. *1012*

Below When opened in 1873 Buccleuch Dock was enclosed at its southern end by an embankment from Salthouse to Barrow Island on which ran a railway line to a pier on Walney Channel. When Ramsden Dock was completed an 80-foot-wide opening joining the two docks was made and the railway was carried over on a single-line swing bridge brought into use in August 1878. By the early 1900s the size and draught of ships being built by Vickers required the widening of the passageways and deepening of the sills of the Barrow Docks, and the Buccleuch Dock opening was increased by 20 feet. At the same time a new Scherzer roll lift bascule bridge was erected by John Aird & Co of Glasgow.

The bridge was built in sections on the dockside and over one weekend, when the dock passage was closed, the new lifting portion was slid into position using barges to support it until it could be riveted together. Opened on 12 October 1908, the bridge was, because of its appearance, known affectionately to Barrovians as the 'Cradle Bridge'. It is seen here in the partly opened position as construction nears completion. Double railway tracks on either side were interlaced so that only a single line crossed the bridge, the space remaining being occupied by a roadway. Declared unsafe because of corrosion in November 1966, it was closed to rail traffic on 31 December of that year. It remained permanently in the raised position for at least another year before being finally demolished. The many-ventilatored roof of the Furness Railway loco shed can be seen in the distance. *537*

Below In the summer of 1935 Orient Line's 20,000-ton passenger liner *Orford* is shepherded through the 8-acre basin of Ramsden Dock on her way to a refit by her builders, Vickers Armstrong Ltd. The gates at the entrance to the dock from Walney Channel can be seen, closed, in the left foreground. Towed by Barrow-based LMS tugs *Devonshire* and *Ramsden*, with two further tugs, owned by the Rea Towing Company of Liverpool, controlling her stern, *Orford*, after threading her way along the basin, will be guided through a lock before entering the main body of the dock, whence she will negotiate the bascule

THE FURNESS RAILWAY

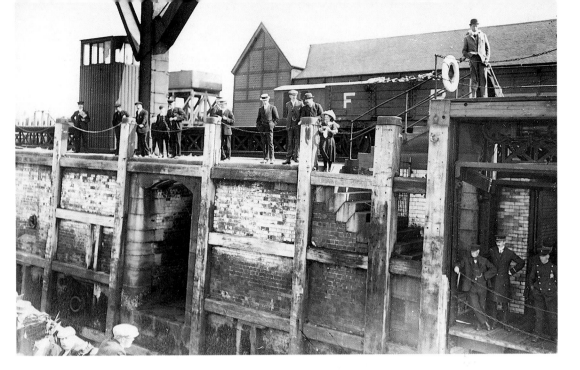

bridge seen above and the high-level bridge seen on page 40 before reaching her berth beneath the 150-ton crane on the Vickers fitting-out wharf in Devonshire Dock. In addition to the main dock area, Ramsden Dock also had a branch known as the Anchor Line basin, the southern side of which was lined by grain sheds. These and the grain elevators associated with them can be seen beyond the dockside cranes to the left of the liner's stern. *A468*

Above Taken from the deck of one of the paddle-steamers at low tide, this view of the Dock Station landing stage beside the entrance to Ramsden Dock shows the different levels at which passengers could land, or embark, depending on the level of the tide. The goods wagon just visible is a 10-ton four-plank type built in the 1880s, of which the Furness Railway had more than 250 available for traffic. *1072*

Below A great deal of railway activity was concentrated in the Ramsden Dock area, and here is an interesting array of goods stock, photographed in early LMS days. Several still carry the names of their pre-Grouping companies, and wagons from the Midland, LNWR, Cleator & Workington and Furness companies can be identified. The vessel in the background is the Furness-Withy Line steamer *Quernmore*, which, with her sister ship *Dromore*, sailed on a service between Barrow and New York from Ramsden Dock. *8137*

Above A reversal of activity at Barrow as iron ore, the original export commodity, is seen here being imported through Ramsden Dock. Cranes are busily unloading ore, probably from Spain, from the holds of a freighter into Furness Railway ore wagons, although the metal-bodied wagon in the middle row could belong to the North Lonsdale Ironworks. The scene is probably during the 1914-18 war when electric cranes, with mechanical grabs, were introduced to save labour and speed up the turn-round of ships. Note the large buckets in the foreground, pivoted below the centre of gravity in order to be self-emptying when a catch securing the handle was disengaged. *CRA, Walker Collection WC17*

Below Another valuable traffic to be imported through Ramsden Dock was pulp timber for use at the Barrow Paper Mills, situated adjacent to the east side of Cavendish Dock, the buildings of which still exist, housing a number of small industries. The timber can be seen in the wagons on the right of the picture and has just been unloaded from a Belgian freighter. Note the three-masted sailing ship in the left background, probably discharging grain, as it appears to be tied up alongside the grain storage sheds in the Anchor Line basin. Grain was sometimes carried to Barrow in sailing ships in pre-1914 days when this photograph was taken. *3017*

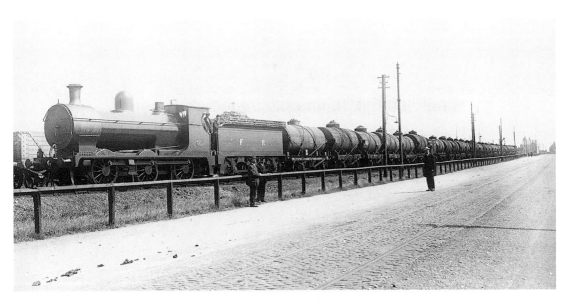

Above A train of oil tank wagons from the Anglo-American Oil Company's installation at Ramsden Dock is posed alongside Ramsden Dock Road, down the centre of which can be seen the single tramway track on which Corporation tramcars travelled between the town and Ramsden Dock station. First laid down in 1886, the tramway was operated by steam trams until 1904, at which time electric traction, managed for Barrow Corporation by the British Electric Traction Company, took over. Immaculate 0-6-0 goods engine No 27, in charge of the train, was one of a batch of 19 such engines entering service between 1913 and 1920, and supplied

variously by Sharp Stewart, Nasmyth Wilson and the North British Locomotive Company. No 27 was built by the latter company, entering service in 1914 and inheriting its number from an 1866-built 0-4-0 tender engine, which then became 27A in the supplementary list. Designed primarily for hauling heavy mineral trains, these engines were frequently used on passenger services, and all lived to be taken into LMS ownership at the Grouping in 1923; the new No 27 became LMS number 12498. Six of these engines even survived to be nationalised in 1948, but No 27 was not one of them, having been scrapped in 1932. *7547*

Above right In common with many other pre-Grouping railway companies, the Furness Railway had its own workshops for the repair of locomotives and rolling-stock, etc. They were situated on land adjacent to Salthouse Road, behind the General Offices. In this view from the clock tower of the Offices, probably in 1924, most of the shops can be identified, the two-storeyed building on the extreme

left being the Machine Shop, and the long single-storey shop to its right the Carriage & Wagon Repair Shop. Next, with a tower over the entrance, is the Carriage & Wagon Construction Shop, adjacent to which, with ventilatored roof, is the Foundry. The Boiler, Erecting and Blacksmith's Shops cannot be seen on this picture, but they were located behind and to the left of the Machine Shop.

Passing into LMS ownership in 1923, the existence of the works was soon under threat as the new owners sought to concentrate all repair work at four main centres, Derby, Crewe, Horwich and Glasgow. The decision to close the Barrow works was made in February 1931 and all repair work for the Furness area was transferred to the former Lancashire & Yorkshire Railway workshops at Horwich. Only the Blacksmith's Shop and main Erecting Shops adjacent to Salthouse Road have survived, now housing car workshops and new car stores; the rest of the site has been cleared and is either occupied by small local industries or derelict. *A189*

Left The advantages of Barrow as a sea-port, protected as it is by the natural sea barrier of Walney Island, soon became apparent to Sir James Ramsden as he pursued his policy of developing the industrial and commercial potential of the region. However, this natural barrier was later to prove something of a disadvantage, as its close proximity to Barrow Island, together with the action of tides sweeping up and down Walney Channel, were to create a silting problem not originally appreciated. It was largely due to the dredging of this silt, which in future years was to prove so costly, that Sir James's dream of Barrow as a port rivalling Liverpool in importance, was never realised.

In 1863 Royal Assent was granted to a Bill transferring the estates of the Barrow Harbour Commissioners to the Furness Railway, giving the Company the power to construct docks. When the four docks at Barrow, owned and operated by the Railway Company, had been completed, they dealt with a considerable amount of shipping traffic of all types, both freight and passenger, including daily sailings to Belfast and, in the summer, to the Isle of Man, by steamers jointly owned by the Furness and Midland companies in conjunction with the Barrow Shipping firm James Little.

All of this activity was controlled from the Harbour Office, which, when the docks entrance was at the northern end of the system, was at the northern end of Devonshire Dock. However, with the opening of Ramsden Dock in 1881 and the transfer of the entrance to the southern end of the system, a new harbour office, seen here, was built on a prominence overlooking Ramsden Dock Road and Walney Channel. Here was the office of the Harbour Master, Admiral Barnett, who was succeeded on his retirement on 31 December 1899 by Captain Wards, and later by Captain Bissett. The Harbour Office is still in use, although the cupola was taken down in about 1975, and the railway lines in the foreground, which carried trains to and from Ramsden Dock Station, have long been lifted. *107*

Below left To maintain the dock walls and gates a team of divers was required by the Railway Company, and here they pose, four strong, together with their supporting personnel, in front of the Sankey camera. They worked from a small support boat, equipped with a hand-operated pump to supply air to the divers as they carried out their underwater tasks. When not in use, the diving boat was moored in Buccleuch Dock close to the High Level Bridge.

The foreman diver, on the left of the front row, Mr 'Willy' Rimmer, was born on 5 March 1873 and joined the Railway Company on 2 December 1905. Along with many staff of a similar status he joined the Company's salaried staff on 1 September 1916 at a salary of £208. In addition the divers received an extra allowance of 2s 6d per hour when actually diving. As well as diving in the docks, Mr Rimmer was occasionally required to dive in such locations as oil tanks, to unblock valves, and in flooded mine workings. *3852*

3.
THE MAIN LINE NORTH
FROM BARROW

In 1854 extensive sidings were laid adjacent to the main line, just north of Thwaite Flat, to serve a new mine working a rich source of iron ore discovered by Henry Schneider at Park, a few miles to the west of Dalton. The sidings were controlled by signal boxes at each end, Park South and Park North. Here No 30, an 0-6-0 mineral engine supplied in 1918 by the North British Locomotive Company, approaches the tall Park South Down Main Distant signal with a mixed goods train on 31 January 1919. Becoming LMS No 12507 at the Grouping, No 30 was scrapped in 1935.

The signal is of special interest as it is fitted with gas lighting, fed from a cylinder which can be seen at the foot of the post. Supplied by the Gas Accumulator Company (UK Ltd), the system was known as the Aga Flashlight Signal, and six units were fitted, free of charge, to the Up and Down Distant signals at Park South, Askam station and Green Road station during 1914 for a trial period of six months. At the end of the trial period the units were purchased for £16 10s 0d cash, less 2½% discount, this information being given to the Traffic & Works Committee at its meeting on Wednesday 25 November 1914. Situated 817 yards from Park South signal box, the signal is on a 29ft 6in post dating from 1908. The winch-operated lamp has been retained, possibly in reserve in case of failure of the gas-powered lamp. Note also the inside-keyed track, probably dating from the opening of the line from Salthouse Junction to Park South on 1 June 1882. *7300*

Above Park South and Park North signal boxes were built to a similar pattern, although that at the south end was slightly larger as it was also responsible for a level crossing carrying the Roanhead to Dalton road over the line and the junction where the 1882-opened Thwaite Flat to Salthouse loop left the line to Dalton. The two boxes, similar in appearance, were to the same design as that at Ramsden Dock station (see Volume 2) and opened in 1883, replacing earlier boxes on the same sites. Park North box and a typical Furness Railway crossing-keeper's house are seen here at the foot of an inclined tramway bringing ore down from the mine to the sidings. Replaced by a ground frame after closure on 11 April 1933, the stone-built base of this box is still in use as a permanent way cabin. The sidings were lifted in 1963 but Park South box is still in operation. *Barrow Library collection*

Above right Askam station, seen here with a down passenger train departing on its way north, is on the original Furness Railway line of 1846. Built to serve a village that developed as a direct result of the establishment of Askam Iron Works in 1867, the station opened on 1 April 1868. The illustrated Paley & Austin-designed station building with its overhanging roof dates from 1877, replacing an earlier wooden structure. The signal box opened on 30 October 1890, the goods yard dates from 1891 and the up platform waiting shelter from 1904. In June 1900 Dalton Urban District Council applied for a footbridge to be built at the level crossing in view of the

number of children crossing the railway, and a plan was submitted for a structure at an estimated cost of £350. The application, made at the same time as that for Lindal, was deferred and the footbridge was never built.

Rail access to the iron works, which closed in the 1930s, left the main line south of Askam station and the junction was controlled by Askam Iron Works signal box. This box survived the closure of the iron works and in latter years serviced a siding laid into the new brickworks during November 1899.

Although now an unstaffed halt, Askam station has changed little today, the major difference being the level crossing, which is now of the lifting barrier type. The goods shed was demolished in the 1970s to make way for industrial units, but the main station waiting room was re-opened for the benefit of passengers, after refurbishment by volunteers, on 2 July 1993. *2145*

Kirkby was the northern extremity of the 1846 Furness Railway line and it was from sidings just north of the station that slate, brought down from the nearby Burlington Slate Quarries by means of a self-acting incline, was transported to Barrow for shipping. This traffic, from quarries owned by the Earl of Burlington, who gave influential and financial backing to the building of the railway, was one of the main reasons for the line's existence. The station buildings pictured here date from 1904 when Kirkby and Ireleth Parish Council complained about the dilapidated state of the accommodation erected in 1848. G. Frearson, builder, of Broughton, carried out the work at a cost of £446 2s 11d.

The signal box was unusual in that, like the structure provided at Furness Abbey (page 25) it was attached to the small waiting shelter on the down platform. Opened on 3 July 1893, this box replaced a ground frame 50 yards away on the up platform that had been provided during February 1886 along with basic signalling. The site of the signal box can still be clearly seen on the north side of the small waiting shelter.

An up passenger train is approaching from the north, but its arrival goes unnoticed as all eyes are turned towards the camera. The famous long seat on the northbound platform, which at one time appeared in *The Guinness Book of Records*, can clearly be seen and traces of it still remain. Now an unstaffed halt, all the main station buildings seen here, with the exception of the down platform waiting shelter, have gone, but Kirkby now boasts a footbridge brought from Lindal and erected at the station following a fatal accident to a passenger crossing the line. *2829*

THE FURNESS RAILWAY

An Act of 1846 permitted the Furness Railway to extend its line northwards from Kirkby to Broughton, and this it did, opening the extension in February 1848.

The Whitehaven & Furness Junction Railway, coming south, formed a trailing connection with the Furness Railway line north of Foxfield, which opened on 1 November 1850, and some eight years later, in 1858, a connecting curve between the two lines was installed forming a triangle, the northern side of which was soon abandoned. At the southern junction a station was built at Foxfield, and in 1866 the two railways amalgamated. The station seen here, dating from 1879, had an island platform, one side, partially covered, serving main-line trains, the other side being used mainly by trains running on the Coniston branch. Adjacent to the covered platform was a goods shed, and the photograph also shows 2-4-2 tank engine No 72 entering the branch platform, bunker first, with a passenger train from Coniston. A signal box was added to the north end of the platform building, which is still in use, although the rest of the station buildings have gone. The Station Master's house on the right, which in early days contained the booking office, is still to be seen, as is the water tank beyond. *4007*

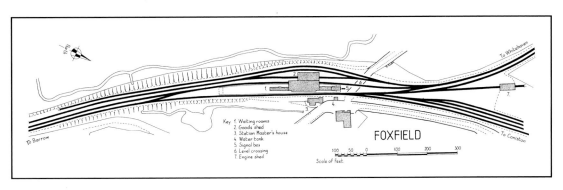

Key 1. Waiting rooms
2. Goods shed
3. Station Master's house
4. Water tank
5. Signal box
6. Level crossing
7. Engine shed

To Barrow

To Whitehaven

To Coniston

FOXFIELD

100 50 0 100 200 300
Scale of feet

Map of Foxfield station. *Mike Faulkner*

Below In 1856 a large deposit of very high-quality haematite iron ore was discovered at Hodbarrow and, when large-scale mining operations began, sidings for the handling of the ore traffic were built at Holborn Hill station on the 1850-opened southern section of the Whitehaven & Furness Junction Railway. The founding of an iron works close to Holborn Hill resulted in the development of a small town, which was named Millom, and Holborn Hill station was incorporated into the town, changing its name to become Millom station. It was a busy station and had extensive sidings to deal with the products from the Hodbarrow mine and the iron works. The station remained much as it is seen here – with an 0-6-2 tank engine entering the down platform

with a passenger train from Barrow – until 1968, when the iron works closed and traffic from it and the mines ceased.

The platform awning on the down (right-hand) platform was taken down and re-erected at the Ravenglass & Eskdale Railway's narrow gauge station at Ravenglass in 1972. That on the up platform, just visible beyond the footbridge, is still in position but with a replacement roof, and the footbridge has lost its sides and roof. The station buildings still stand but are not in use, and passengers in both directions are protected from the elements in bus-type shelters. Recently the main station building on the Barrow-bound platform has been refurbished and converted to craft workshops and similar enterprises. *5967*

Above right Silecroft is another of the stations on the Whitehaven & Furness Junction Railway, a line that was constructed on a very tight monetary budget. This was reflected in the poor quality of the various structures, most of which, including the viaducts, were built of wood and many of which had to be replaced by the Furness Railway Company after it had taken over the line. It is possible that the wooden buildings at Silecroft station seen in this photograph were relics from the original company. The view is looking north towards Whitehaven. *2612*

Right This is Silecroft station after a facelift undertaken by the Furness Company – even the sleepers of the crossing have been replaced. The signal box is, however, unchanged and remained in this form until 1923 when it was rebuilt and relocated to the opposite side of the station just south of the level crossing. In January 1907 Mr W. B. Walker of Kellet House, Silecroft, submitted an application for the spelling of the station name to be altered to the old style of Sylecroft, but the FR Board decided to leave the spelling as it had been for 50 years, and that is how it remains today. *5531*

THE MAIN LINE NORTH FROM BARROW 55

Above The typical Furness Railway station building at Bootle, seen here looking north towards Whitehaven, was one of several built to a design by the Lancaster firm of architects Paley & Austin, erected in 1873 at the time when the hitherto single Whitehaven & Furness Junction Railway track was doubled, the date being commemorated in cast iron on the station building downspouts. This was a frequently used design and can be seen in the pictures of Ravenglass and Drigg on the Barrow to Whitehaven line, as well as at Greenodd and Haverthwaite on the Lakeside branch. All except Greenodd still exist, but none are now in railway ownership. The other buildings, signal box and goods shed, are also typical of those erected as standard at country stations, and all the buildings seen in the photograph still remain although the main station house, now a private dwelling, is fenced off from the platform.

Following a fatal accident to a passenger named Bushby when crossing the line on 23 May 1907, the Board of Trade asked for consideration to be given to the provision of a footbridge or subway, but the Railway Company, through its Traffic & Works Committee, decided 'that the ordinary business of Bootle does not justify the erection of a footbridge'.

It is interesting to note that the village of Bootle is situated nearly a mile inland from the railway, and an independent cluster of houses that grew around the railway station is known as Bootle Station. *2338*

Above right A snowdrift at Bootle station has blocked the line and this photograph shows a works train with a snow-clearing gang waiting at the north end of the station while the men get to grips with re-opening the route. The train includes a standard Furness Railway goods brake-van. The interesting engineers' riding van, marshalled in front of the brake-van, appears to be a conversion from an early five-compartment coach. *2356*

Right On the other side of the train, looking from the down platform in the direction of Whitehaven, we see the gang engaged in the task of the clearing the snow from the tracks and loading it into the wagons behind the 0-6-0 goods engine. Prominent at the end of the platform is the station signal box, still in use today albeit equipped with a modern British Railways-designed frame, brought from Nethertown when that box closed in 1970 (see page 65). The typical Furness Railway Down Home signal has a winch-operated lamp at the foot of the post. The arm would be coloured red with a white band. *2343*

THE FURNESS RAILWAY

THE MAIN LINE NORTH FROM BARROW

Below Eskmeals station, opened in 1850 and closed in 1960, showing interesting rolling-stock with an engineers' van similar to that just seen in Bootle station. Beyond the station the line passes over the estuary of the River Esk on a 297-yard-long viaduct, built in 1867 by the Furness Railway with stone piers to replace the original wooden structure of the Whitehaven & Furness Junction Railway. The illuminated speed restriction sign on the down line at the platform end, which limits train speeds over the viaduct to 45mph, is also of interest; the Furness Company was a pioneer of this type of sign, which alerted drivers to restrictions even during the hours of darkness. Interesting too are the Home signals in the distance mounted back to back on a single post, a standard arrangement for stations without signal boxes. Similar signals could be seen at Braystones further north and at Heversham on the Hincaster branch. The down (left-hand) platform waiting shelter was erected in 1902 at a cost of £40, after residents had complained about having to wait for northbound trains on the up platform in wet weather.

South of Eskmeals was a gun-proving range belonging to Vickers, on which naval guns were proof tested. This was served by a siding off the main down line, controlled by a signal box that was taken down on 22 November 1992 for preservation by a local railway enthusiast. Works personnel travelling to and from the gun range were catered for at a wooden halt platform named Monk Moors, erected in 1901, where trains would stop, on request, for their convenience. *2981*

Above right Ravenglass station opened in 1849 when the Whitehaven & Furness Junction Railway reached this point on its way south to join with the Furness Railway at Broughton. The track was doubled in 1872 after the Furness Company acquired the line, which allowed the station as seen here to be constructed in 1873. This view was taken from the up platform looking in the direction of Barrow, with 4-4-0 passenger engine No 126 in the offset down platform heading a train for Whitehaven. A 1901 introduction, this Sharp Stewart-built locomotive was scrapped in 1931 carrying LMS number 10143.

The typical Furness Railway country station goods shed can be seen beyond the platform end, while in the background are the tall signal box and the footbridge that carried, and indeed still does carry, passengers alighting from trains from the south across the tracks to the Ravenglass & Eskdale Railway (featured in Volume 2). This footbridge, although maintained by the railway and allocated FR Bridge No 146, is not a station footbridge as such, but was constructed to carry a public footpath over the railway. *5153*

Right We are now looking towards Whitehaven from the footbridge visible in the background of the previous picture. In the up platform locomotive No 131, introduced in 1913 and one of the final batch of 4-4-0 passenger engines, waits with a train for Barrow for a busy interchange of passengers. Stored on the siding leading to the goods shed is a 1906-built cattle van, its lower sides liberally coated with lime, while on the down line an up goods train, running wrong line, is waiting for the passenger train to clear the station before crossing to its correct road.

All buildings in this scene still exist, passing into the ownership of the Ravenglass & Eskdale Railway when British Railways made Ravenglass an unmanned halt in 1967. The main station building is now the 'Ratty Arms', the goods shed is a workshop and the up platform waiting shelter now houses a museum. *5662*

Below Until the building of the 3-foot-gauge line along the Esk valley from Boot to Ravenglass in 1875, Drigg was the port from which iron ore, mined at the head of the valley, was shipped after being carted some 10 miles to the coast. The up platform at Drigg, seen here in Furness Railway days, shows to advantage the Paley & Austin-designed building, with the station house on the left and the booking office and waiting rooms on the right. The advertisements on the station wall are interesting and reflect the era during which the photograph was taken. Roans of Whitehaven are makers of saddlery, harness and leggings; the *North Western Daily Mail* cost just one half-penny; R. F. Case & Co were brewers at Ulverston and Barrow; and Veno's Cough Cure and Mazawattee Tea are also featured. *5598*

Above right Here is a 1914-18 wartime picture of Seascale station (note the partially blacked-out platform lamps) with a Barrow-bound passenger train from Whitehaven arriving in the charge of 4-4-0 locomotive No 37. An 1896 introduction built by Sharp Stewart, No 37 lived on until being scrapped as LMS No 10036 in 1931.

Seascale was just a tiny hamlet when the Whitehaven & Furness Junction Railway reached there in 1849, and that Company attempted to promote the village as a holiday resort in conjunction with the privately owned Scafell Hotel, which had been built adjacent to the railway in 1857. The Furness Railway, when it took over the line in 1866, continued with the village's development, purchasing a large tract of land in 1870 on which it set about building what it termed 'the Eastbourne of the North', plans for which included a Grand Hotel, promenade and marine walk. Work started in 1879 but foundered partly in the face of stiff opposition from local residents, but mostly because the expected flood of visitors never materialised. Seascale did, however, become the Company's number two resort, its first being Grange-over-Sands, and the station was the interchange point from rail to road transport for passengers booked on the Furness

Railway's Wastwater tour. This activity, however, did not please local residents either, even if it did bring in a certain amount of trade, and in June 1905 they complained to the Company stating 'the numbers of excursionists assembling on the sea-front, and consequent ice-cream carts, piano organs and cyclists, constitute a nuisance.' *5926*

Right This view of the down platform buildings at Seascale station from the seaward side of the railway features the Company's 'Refreshment Pavilion Overlooking the Sea' advertised at the ticket barrier on Barrow station (see page 29). Built in 1913, when one of the refreshment houses in the village was closed, this commodious building housed, in addition to the refreshment room itself, a kitchen, two bedrooms for the staff and ladies' toilet facilities. Managed for the Railway Company by Spiers & Pond, the venture cost £970 to build. It was constructed on the northbound platform because a deed of 1856 prevented the erection of any building on the landward side of the station without the consent of the then owner of the Scafell Hotel, one John Tyson, or any of his heirs. Mrs Tyson, the owner in 1913, used this deed to prevent the building of the refreshment

THE FURNESS RAILWAY

room on the up platform, but was powerless to stop it being erected on the down side. Had the Railway Company purchased the hotel when it was offered to it in 1901, this problem would not have arisen. As it was the platform had to be widened and lengthened in order to accommodate the new structure, which was additional to the existing waiting shelter. The building has a 'new' look here suggesting that the photograph was possibly taken in 1913. *4879*

Above A post-Great War scene at Seascale (note that the lamp black-outs have now been removed) with, once again, an up passenger train hauled this time by 4-4-0 locomotive No 129 of 1901, soon to become LMS No 10146. Several changes can be seen when this photograph is compared with the upper view on the previous page; the refreshment pavilion has disappeared and the down platform building is considerably reduced in size. In addition, the down platform has been lengthened and a footbridge connecting the two platforms installed.

On numerous occasions the Company had discussed the provision of either a footbridge or a subway between the platforms at Seascale station, and in 1916 plans were formulated for the construction of a subway costing £2,100, work to start at the end of the war. In the event the cost must have proved too great, and a footbridge was provided instead, which has now been demolished. Only the very wide platform on the down side still shows where the 'Refreshment Pavilion Overlooking the Sea' once stood. *6419*

Below Map of Seascale station. *Mike Faulkner*

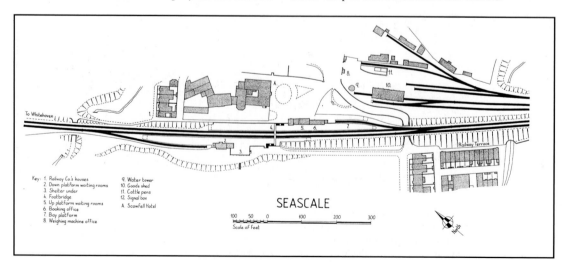

Key: 1. Railway Co's houses
2. Down platform waiting rooms
3. Shelter under
4. Footbridge
5. Up platform waiting rooms
6. Booking office
7. Bay platform
8. Weighing machine office
9. Water tower
10. Goods shed
11. Cattle pens
12. Signal box
A. Scawfell Hotel

SEASCALE

100 50 0   100   200   300
Scale of Feet

To Whitehaven

Railway Terrace

From a camera position north of Seascale station the main line is seen following the coast, in a northerly direction, towards Sellafield. On its way it passes beneath an attractive cast iron accommodation bridge carrying a footpath over the railway from the village to the sea-shore. As with the bridge at Ravenglass station (see page 59) the Seascale footbridge has no railway connection, but in common with all bridges that cross the railway it is allocated a bridge number, in this instance 161. The crossing still exists, but the illustrated bridge has been replaced by a different structure. *5591A*

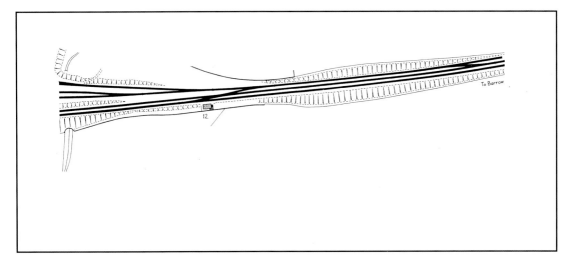

Below In Furness Railway days Sellafield station was the interchange point between the southern end of the Whitehaven, Cleator & Egremont Railway and the Furness north-south main line. Opened in 1857 to connect the mines in the Cleator area with the port of Whitehaven, the link with Sellafield was not made until 1869, and the WC&ER was annexed jointly by the LNWR and Furness Railway in 1878. This photograph, looking south through the station, was probably taken in the late 1950s, by which time some sections of the WC&ER line had already closed,

services into Sellafield ending at the beginning of 1970. The Furness main line operated on either side of the island platform beyond the signal box and the line to Egremont ran from the bay on the left of the picture. The major passenger traffic nowadays is local passenger trains between Barrow and Carlisle, and workmen's services to and from the nearby works of British Nuclear Fuels Ltd. The cottages in the foreground were demolished in January 1990. *Author's collection*

Above right As built, the Whitehaven & Furness Junction Railway Company's line was single track only, but acquisition by the Furness Company resulted in the doubling of the line as far as Sellafield in 1873-74. From there northwards the railway, passing through stations serving the villages of Braystones, Nethertown and St Bees, hugs the coast for several miles, and the track was allowed to remain single, only being doubled for passing purposes in the stations at Nethertown and St Bees.

Braystones station is seen here from the seashore, and being the only station on the single-track section not doubled for passing, it had just a single platform. The Up and Down Home signals carried on a single lattice post, as at Eskmeals (page 58), were operated by the station staff from a ground frame. The station building, which is little more than a crossing-keeper's house, is today a burnt-out shell.

Station Mistress Mrs McGill, who had been at Braystones for 33 years earning 10 shillings a week, retired in November 1907, and as women employees were not

eligible to receive superannuation, the Board granted her a retirement gratuity of £50. *E913*

Right This distant view of Nethertown station, with the Station Master's house (featured in the television series *A Family at War*) prominent on the seaward side, shows the single track winding its way northwards beyond the station and along the coast towards St Bees. At the start of the First World War, in August 1914, the 126-yard-long passing loop at Nethertown held 21 standard length wagons. A memo of April 1916 to the Company's Traffic & Works Committee described the delays this was causing to the increased traffic resulting from wartime conditions. Mr Haynes, the Superintendent of the Line, recommended that the existing loop be extended by 68 yards, at a cost of £300, to accommodate the longer trains being run. He also pointed out that a further extension would shortly be needed, but suggested that the work be carried out as a separate scheme to keep initial costs down. These proposals were evidently disregarded, as the Traffic &

THE FURNESS RAILWAY

Works Committee, at its meeting on 31 May 1916, approved an expenditure of £160 to extend the shunting neck, and give additional siding accommodation of 90 yards, to ease the problems. The loop and siding were demolished in 1970 leaving only a single line through the station. *H225*

Below The most northerly of the villages along the Furness main line to be promoted as a holiday resort, St Bees can trace its origins back to the time of the Norman Conquest. Dominated by St Bees Head on the seaward side of the railway, the village is the home of St Bees School. Comprising only this school, a priory and one street when the railway first arrived, a large and commodious hotel was soon built, hoping to attract business from the new railway. By 1857 the village was expanding rapidly, although the hotel never achieved its object and later became Grindle House, one of the halls of residence for boarders at the School. North from St Bees the line continued to be single until Mirehouse Junction, just south of Whitehaven, where the Whitehaven, Cleator & Egremont Railway's line

joined, to run alongside the Furness line to Whitehaven Corkickle.

In this illustration the Barrow-bound train in the up platform is headed by 4-6-4 'Baltic' tank engine No 115, the number originally carried by the 0-6-0 goods engine lost in the Lindal subsidence of 1892 (see page 23). This new 115, allocated LMS No 11100 in 1923, was scrapped in 1935. *6550*

Bottom One of two stations at Whitehaven, Corkickle was 74 miles from Carnforth via Barrow – the 74 milepost is on the platform a few yards short of the tunnel. Originally the northern end of the Whitehaven & Furness Junction Railway, that Company was authorised in 1847 to build a line from Whitehaven Preston Street to join with the Furness Railway, then under construction, at Broughton, which it eventually did in 1850 (see page 53).

The connection northwards from Corkickle, with the 1847-opened Whitehaven Junction Railway running between Whitehaven Bransty and the Maryport & Carlisle Railway at Maryport, was by means of a tortuous link through the rail system of the Whitehaven docks until a tunnel, between Corkickle and Bransty, was opened in 1852. The southern portal of this single-track 74-chain (1,628-yard) tunnel can be seen in this late 1930s picture. Corkickle was also the northern end of the Whitehaven, Cleator & Egremont

THE FURNESS RAILWAY

Railway, and had extensive goods sidings, a busy goods yard and a small engine shed with coaler. All except the station have now gone; trains still call at the unmanned halt and the platform building is there, without its canopy and not in railway use. *CRA, Pattinson Collection PA0225*

Above The other Whitehaven station was Bransty, and this view along platform 2, the arrival platform for trains from Barrow, shows an ex-Lancashire & Yorkshire Railway engine, LMS No 12091, emerging from the northern end of Whitehaven tunnel in a cloud of smoke on 30 August 1939. The picture gives some indication of the conditions endured by the crews of steam locomotives passing through the tunnel, despite four ventilation shafts. The merging of the tracks before entering the tunnel can clearly be seen, and the presence of a 5mph speed restriction indicates that the tunnel was in the process of being rebuilt when the picture was taken. The work was carried out at night to minimise disruption to traffic and at the same time make working conditions better for the reconstruction gangs. The alterations took some 21 years to complete and were not finished until 1958. Bransty No 1 signal box closed on 25 April 1965. *Author's collection*

Below This wider view of Bransty station, taken from a DMU departing from platform 2 for Workington on 29 June 1959, shows the Barrow-bound platform 3 on the left and the ex-LNWR platform 1 (the LNWR having annexed the Whitehaven Junction Railway in 1866) on the extreme right. The splendid awnings and station building have now been replaced by more spartan passenger accommodation. *Author's collection*

4.
BRANCH LINES

Kendal branch

This 5-mile-long branch, which linked the Furness Railway main line at Arnside with the LNWR's West Coast Main line at Hincaster, a few miles south of Oxenholme, eventually gave the FR access to the latter's branch to Kendal.

Opened on 26 June 1876, this was a single track, doubled only at the stations at Arnside and Sandside. It was constructed primarily to enable coke, produced in the South Durham coalfields, to be transported to the ironworks at Ulverston, Barrow, Askam and Millom, without the need for coke trains to trundle

further south to Carnforth and pass through the busy exchange sidings there. The coke trains crossed the Pennines on the South Durham & Lancashire Union Railway line, which ran from West Auckland via Barnard Castle and the 1,370-foot Stainmore summit to Tebay. Here they were picked up in exchange sidings by Furness locomotives and carried south for a short distance over the LNWR main line before joining the Furness branch at Hincaster Junction.

Passenger traffic on the Hincaster branch developed when the Furness Railway Company obtained running rights over LNWR metals to run services from Grange to Kendal via Oxenholme and the Windermere branch. Known locally as 'Kendal Tommy', this was the regular passenger service over the branch, there being six trains in each direction daily in 1914, and these were used by day pupils attending Heversham School, who travelled from as far afield as Grange and Kendal. Another regular passenger working was a fortnightly special train carrying Durham mine workers to and from their convalescent home at Conishead Priory (see Bardsea branch, page 92).

Left 'Kendal Tommy', the name by which the branch-line train to Kendal was always known, in the charge of an unidentified 2-4-2 tank engine, has just left Arnside and is running alongside the River Kent estuary towards Sandside some time between 1914, when the Arnside platform building was re-built, and 1924, when the last of the 2-4-2 tanks was scrapped. *W. Anderson collection*

Above The Kendal branch left the Furness Railway main line from a platform on the up side at Arnside station, and this circa 1900 view from the branch shows the mock-Tudor-style platform building to advantage (see also page 10). On the left are the main-line down platform building and waiting shelter, which also contained the Station Master's house until it was rebuilt in the goods yard in 1906. The small bridge in the centre carried a short siding to the goods yard. *Author's collection*

Sandside was one of the two intermediate stations on the branch. The station building was a striking edifice, in a 'Swiss chalet' style with overhanging roof; designed by Paley & Austin, it owed its existence to George Edward Wilson, owner of nearby Dallam Tower, who was influential enough to have his demands met for a station close to his residence.

Following the withdrawal of the South Durham coke trains, the Hincaster branch was closed north of Sandside in September 1963, but traffic from a nearby quarry kept the remainder open for another seven years, until final closure on 31 January 1971. The station was demolished and the site is now occupied by a restaurant. *2113*

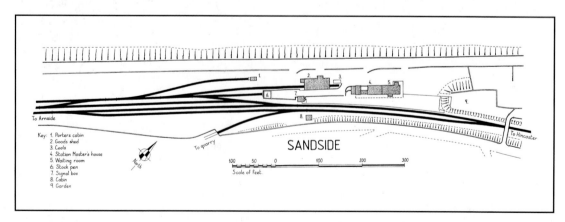

Map of Sandside station. *Mike Faulkner*

THE FURNESS RAILWAY

A splendid portrait of the single-platform Sandside station at the turn of the century. Sandside closed to passenger traffic on 24 May 1942. *Late G. Taylor collection*

Above Shortly after leaving Sandside the branch crossed the Bela River, where it joins the estuary of the River Kent, on the imposing Bela (sometimes Beela) Viaduct (not to be confused with the Belah Viaduct on the Stainmore line). It was a massive structure to carry a single-track branch line over quite a small river, with three steel spans and lengthy, arched stone viaducts, approached by embankments on either side. The reason for the stone structures on each side of the steel spans, instead of earth embankments, was to appease the owner of Dallam Tower, who insisted that solid embankments would spoil the outlook from his windows. In this panoramic view Sandside is to the left, while on the right the line can be seen passing under an overbridge on its way to Heversham station. The viaduct was demolished in the mid-1960s shortly after the line was closed beyond Sandside, but the embankments can still be easily recognised. *Author's collection*

Above right This photograph, taken from the A6 trunk road between Heversham village and Milnthorpe, shows the single line running south along an embankment towards the Bela Viaduct and Sandside. This very steeply graded portion of the branch climbed from sea level at Sandside to nearly 200 feet at Heversham in only 2 miles.

Heversham, the second of the two intermediate stations, was situated just off the right-hand side of the picture. The station signals, two arms on a common post, can be seen on the right, and these were operated by station staff from a ground frame on the platform. The signal arms are interesting, being of two different designs; the down signal, showing its rear side, is a conventional lower-quadrant arm, while the up signal, showing its face, has a spectacle

placed in front of the pivot with a balance weight to the rear. The second arm was installed on 15 October 1892, together with a similar attachment to the up signal post, and at the same time Heversham station was made into a block post employing a single-line staff-and-ticket system to Hincaster Junction in one direction and Sandside in the other. The Furness Company, always economical, re-used the beechwood staff from the Lakeside and Haverthwaite section for the newly created Heversham to Hincaster Junction section, after the Tyers No 6 Tablet system had been installed on the branch to Lakeside. *RS4*

Right This fine portrait of the tiny station at Heversham is looking towards Hincaster and the junction with the LNWR main line. The station was opened on 1 July 1890, and comprised a single platform with a wooden building standing on a brick-built plinth. The bridge at the end of the platform carries the main A6 road between Kendal and Milnthorpe and the one beyond takes a minor road from Heversham village across the railway on its way towards Kirby Lonsdale. Note the typical Furness Railway station nameboard and 'squirrel and grapes' platform seat. The scene can be roughly dated by an extension, of 1904, at the near end of the building to house luggage and bicycles.

A proposal in 1900 to build a goods yard at Heversham station foundered when Capt Bagot of Levens Hall, owner of the land, asked a price of £3 per acre; this meant that the cost of the new yard, including a loop siding on the main line, would be in the region of £1,776, which was considered too much. Passenger services were withdrawn from Heversham station on 24 May 1942. *Late G. Taylor collection*

THE FURNESS RAILWAY

The Kendal branch, or Hincaster branch as it is sometimes known, joined the LNWR's West Coast Main Line at Hincaster Junction, controlled by the typical LNWR signal box shown in this late-1930s photograph. The West Coast line sweeps off the picture on the left and the branch breaks away to its right. *CRA, Pattinson Collection 296*

Lakeside branch

The Lakeside branch was officially opened to traffic on 1 June 1869, although goods traffic had operated as far as Greenodd since March of that year. The building of the line was prompted largely by the tourist traffic potential created when the Railway Company acquired a share in the Windermere United Steam Yacht Company, which operated three small passenger steamers, *Firefly*, *Dragonfly* and *Rothay* on Windermere Lake from a landing stage at Newby Bridge. Revenue was also anticipated from the iron works and dye works at Backbarrow, together with traffic expected to generate from the gunpowder factories at Haverthwaite and Black

Above right Greenodd station was built virtually on the seashore and the down platform shelter had rear windows to allow waiting passengers to look out over the Leven estuary. The up platform building, constructed in a rather garish yellow-coloured brick with purple-black banding, was to the Paley & Austin design used on several other Furness Railway country stations. (Curiously, this branch

Beck. The Midland Railway too, having gained access to the Furness network at Carnforth via the Wennington branch, was anxious to have an outlet into the Lake District to compete with the London & North Western Railway's Windermere branch, and encouraged the project.

Access to the branch from Barrow and the north was gained at Plumpton Junction, some 1½ miles from Ulverston, while trains from Carnforth joined at Leven Junction, just north of the Leven Viaduct. Engineered to take double track along its full length, this facility extended only as far as Greenodd; thereafter the line was single, except for a short double section at Haverthwaite, for passing purposes.

was 'Up Line' to Lakeside.) Freight traffic was served by a small goods shed and yard to the south of the station. *5317*

Right In its heyday Greenodd was quite a busy little station; the Summer Timetable for 1914 (about the date of the photograph above) shows 25 passenger trains calling there on weekdays, and six on Sundays.

Windermere Branch and Lake Steamers with Connections. 3

WEEK DAYS. / SUNDAYS.

	1	2	3	4	5	6	7	8	9	10	11	12	13	14	15	16	17	18	19	1	2	3	4	5
	a m	a m	a m	a m	a m	a m	p m	p m	p m	p m	p m	p m	p m	p m	p m					no'n	p m	p m	p m	p m
Grasmere ....dep	Till Sept. 19th only.	..	7 45	8 30	10 0	11 25	..	..	1 45	3 20	3 20	4 20	5 10	5 10	6 15	..	..	..	..	12 3	2 0	4 25	4 25	6 15
Ambleside .... ,,		..	8 25	9 10	10 55	12 15	1D15	..	2 45	4 5	4 5	4 45	5 10	6 0	0 D15	..	..	..	..	12 5	2 5	4 30	4 30	6 20
Lowwood† .... ,,		..	8 30	9 15	11 0	12 20	1D20	..	2 50	4 10	4 10	5 15	5 6	5 7	D20	..	..	..	..	12 30	2 30	4 55	4 55	6 45
Bowness .... ,,		..	8 55	9 40	11 25	12 45	1D40	..	3 15	4 35	4 35	5 40	6 30	6 35	7D45	..	..	..	..	12 35	2 35	5 0	5 0	6 50
Ferry .... ,,		..	9 0	9 45	11 30	12 50	..	..	3 20	4 40	4 40	5 45	6 35	6 35	7D50	..	..	..	..	12 40	2 40	5 5	5 5	6 55
Storrs† .... ,,		..	9 5	9 50	11 35	12 55	..	..	3 25	4 45	4 45	5 50	6 40	6 40	7D55	..	..	..	..	1 10	3 10	5 35	5 35	7 25
Lake Side, Windermere ...... { arr		..	9 35	10 20	12 5	1 25	..	..	3 55	5	5 25	5 35	6 20	7 10	7 10	8D25	..	..	..	..					
		7 0	8 35	9 40	10 25	12 15	1 35	..	3 35	4	5	5 25	5 35	6 30	7 35	7 15	8D35	..	..	..	..	A	A	A	7 35
Newby Bridge Platform ...... ,,		A	A	A	A	A	A	..	..	..	..	..	..	A	A	A	D	..	..	..	A	A	A	A
Haverthwaite .... ,,		7 8	8 43	9 48	10 33	12 23	1 43	..	3 43	..	..	5 43	6 38	..	7 23	8D43	..	..	..	..	4 53	..	6 3	7 43
Greenodd .... ,,		7 15	8 50	9 55	10 40	12 30	1 50	..	3 50	..	..	5 50	6 45	..	7 30	8D50	..	..	..	..	5 0	..	6 10	7 50
ULVERSTON .... arr		7 25	9 0	10 5	10 50	12 40	2 0	..	4 0	4 24	..	6 0	6 55	..	7 40	9 D 0	..	..	..	..	5 10	6 5	6 20	8 0
Grange .... arr		7 52	9 37	10 35	11 18	1 12	2 42	..	4 27	..	6 2	6 32	7 35	8 6	8 32	9 A35	..	..	..	..	5 37			8 32
Carnforth .... ,,		8 20	10 5	11 0	11 35	1 40	3 10	..	4 55	5	6 32	7 0	7 52	8 32	9 0	9 52	..	..	..	..	6 5	..		9 0
Dalton .... ,,		8 5	9 20	10 35	..	12 59	2 30	..	4 20	5 10	..	6 18	7 25	..	..	9 40	..	..	..	..	6 17	6 35	8 15
Furness Abbey .... ,,		8 15	9 25	10 40	..	1 4	2 35	..	4 25	5 15	..	6 23	7 30	..	..	9 45	..	..	..	..	6 22	6 40	8 20
Barrow Central .... ,,		8 20	9 35	10 50	..	1 11	2 45	..	4 35	5 25	..	6 50	7 40	..	8 10	9 55	..	..	..	..	6 30	6 50	8 30
Foxfield .... ,,		8 49	..	11 34	..	1 36	3 16	..	5 3	6 5	..	..	8 11	..	..	11k26	..	..	..	..	7 21		
Coniston .... ,,		9 25	..	12 20	..	2 10	3 45	..	5 35	6 55	..	..	8 40	..	..	..	..	..	..	..	7 50		
Millom .... ,,		9 3	..	11 26	..	1 48	3 31	..	5 14	6T18	..	..	8 23	..	..	8 43 11k38	..	..	..	..	7 36		
Seascale .... ,,		9 40	..	11 52	..	2 19	4 10	..	5 47	6H43	..	..	..	..	9 20	..	..	..	..	..	8 15		
Whitehaven, Bransty .... ,,		10 7	..	12 20	..	2 53	4 45	..	6 17	7H10	..	..	..	..	9 50	..	..	..	..	8 50		

† Calls when required only. **A** Stops when required to set down passengers on informing the guard at the preceding stopping station, and by signal to take up passengers. **D** Till September 19th only. **H** Commencing July 13th. **S** Saturdays only. **T** 6-35 p.m. July 1st to 11th.

For other connections see page 1.

WEEK DAYS. / SUNDAYS.

	1	2	3	4	5	6	7	8	9	10	11	12	13	14	15	16	17	18	19	1	2	3	4	5
	a m	a m	a m	a m	a m	no'n	a m	a m	a m	p m	p m	p m	p m	p m	p m	p m				a m	p m	p m	p m	p m
Whitehaven, Bransty ....dep	Till Sept. 19th only.	..	6 40	..	10	15	11*25	11 25	..	..	2 40	..	3 35	..	7 30	..	..	..	8 30				
Seascale .... ,,		Thurs and Fri days excepted	7 14	..	10	49	11*55	..	..	..	3 6	..	8 0	..	..	..	9 4				
Millom .... ,,		6 25	9 0	..	11	30	12*26	12 23	..	..	3 38	..	4 50	..	8 26	..	..	..	9 45				
Coniston .... ,,		7 30	8 40	..	11	5	11*50	..	..	..	2 25	..	4 15	6 0	6 25	..	..	..	9 0	C			
Foxfield .... ,,		8 7	9 12	..	11	42	12*35	..	18S	..	2 57	..	5 2	6 22	7 7	..	..	..	9 57				
Barrow Central .... ,,		7 0	8 50	9 45	12C0	12	20	1* 0	12 155	1 50	..	4 10	..	5 40	6 52	9 0	..	..	..	10 30	12 25	2 15	4 45
Furness Abbey .... ,,		7 10	8 55	9 53	12 10	12	30	..	2 0	..	4 15	..	5 50	7 0	7 50	..	..	..	10 40	1B30	2 25	4 55
Dalton .... ,,		7 15	9 0	9 58	..	12	35	..	2 5	..	4 20	..	5 55	7 5	7 55	..	..	..	10 45	..	2 30	5 0
Carnforth .... ,,		7 0	8 15	9 30	10 0	12	15	12 20	12 20	1 33	..	3 48	E53	5 32	7 23	8 35	..	..	..	10 19	..	..	..
Grange .... dep		8 24	8 40	9 55	10 22	12	31	12 45	12 45	1 50	1 58	..	4 44	30	6 3	6 45	9 0	..	..	10 35	..	..	..
ULVERSTON .... dep	8F 0	..	9 10	10 30	..	12	26	12 55	..	1 27	2 25	..	3 25	4 45	5 25	6 35	7 55	9F30	..	11 5	1 46	2 45	5 20
Greenodd .... ,,	8F 7	Till August 31st only.	9 19	10 39	10 47	..	1 4	1 36	..	2 34	2 27	3 34	4 54	5 34	6 44	8 4	9F39	..	11 14	..	2 54	5 29
Haverthwaite .... ,,	6F16		9 28	10 46	..	..	1 11	1 43	..	2 41	..	3 41	5 1	5 41	6 51	8 11	9F46	..	11 21	..	3 1	5 36
Newby Bridge Platform ...... ,,	A F		A	A	A	..	A	A	..	A	..	A	A	A	A	A	A F	..	A		A	A
Lake Side, Windermere ...... { arr	8F25	9 2	9 35	10 55	11 0	12 45	1 20	1 52	..	2 50	2 40	3 50	5 20	..	7F 5	8 20	9F55	..	11 30	2 5	3 10	5 45
	8F35		9 45	11 0	11 10	12 55	1 25	..	2 0	3 25	3 0	4 0	5 45	..	7F30	..	..	..	12 0	2 10	3 45	5 55
Storrs† .... ,,	9F 0	Till August 31st only.	10 0	11 15	11 25	11 35	1 55	..	3 30	3 30	4 20	6 0	..	7F35	..	..	..	12 10	2 45	3 50	6 25
Ferry .... ,,	9F 5		10 5	11 20	11 30	12 1F45	2 10	..	2 35	3 35	3 40	6 5	..	7F40	..	..	..	12 15	2 50	3 55	6 30
Bowness .... ,,	9F15		10 25	11 40	11 50	1F45	2 10	..	3 40	3 40	6 0	..	7F45	..	..	..	12 20	2 55	4 0	6 35
Lowwood† .... ,,	9F15		10 45	12 0	12 10	7F 5	2 30	..	4 0	4 0	6 20	..	8F 5	..	..	..	12 40	3 15	4 20	6 55
Ambleside .... arr	9 45		10 55	12 10	12 20	2F15	2 40	3 0	4 10	4 10	6 30	..	8F15	..	..	..	12 45	3 20	4 25	7 0
Grasmere .... ,,	10 30		11 35	10	..	1	7 15	..	3 50	4 40	..	7 0	..	..	..	12 50	3 25	4 30	7 5

† Calls when required only. **A** Stops when required to set down passengers on informing the guard at the preceding stopping station, and by signal when required to take up passengers. **B** Fleetwood Boat Train.—Arrives Furness Abbey at 12-34 p.m. **C** Ramsden Dock Station. **E** Leaves at 4-0 p.m. until July 11th. **F** Till September 19th only. **S** Saturdays only. ***** July 1st to July 11th only. **‡** Commencing July 13th.

For other connections see page 1.

Above This roadside view of Greenodd station, with an early motor car driving on a carriageway that displays plenty of evidence of the horse-drawn traffic of the day, shows the coloured brickwork and banding to advantage, as well as the station forecourt which, in Furness Railway days, was used by horse-drawn charabancs in connection with tours embracing Coniston Lake. Tour No 2, the Inner Circular Tour, and Tour No 4 the Middle Circular Tour, both used Greenodd as the interchange point between rail and road transport, the former proceeding to Lake Bank by road before sailing along the lake on one of the steamers, and returning to the starting point by rail from Coniston station. This tour also included a visit to Furness Abbey. Participants on Tour No 4 took to the road again at Coniston after sailing on the lake, and were transported by charabanc to Ambleside, where one of the Windermere steam yachts took them to Lakeside station and a train back to the starting point. More details of Furness Railway

THE FURNESS RAILWAY

tours and excursions are given in Volume 2.

Winter timetables on the branch were withdrawn in 1939, but Greenodd remained in summer use until the end of the 1946 Summer timetable, when passenger trains ceased to call. Improvements to the A590 trunk road between Barrow and Levens Bridge, which included construction of a dual carriageway at Greenodd, resulted in demolition of the station building in 1974, and all that now remains is the lower part of the up platform wall incorporated into the lay-by on the Barrow-bound carriageway. The quiet road seen here now carries only traffic travelling away from Barrow. *5343*

Below left No 21, an 0-6-0 tank engine, heads a passenger train from Lakeside across the viaduct at Greenodd that carried the branch line over the confluence of the Crake and Leven rivers. By an interesting coincidence this engine carries the same number as the 2-2-2 well tank locomotive that hauled the inaugural train at the official opening of the branch on 1 June 1869. Leaving Barrow at 7.30am and calling at Ulverston at 8.00am, a local newspaper report of the event records that the train carried 'a goodly number of passengers'. The engine is described as being 'beautifully decorated with evergreens, flowers, banners bearing the National Insignia, Union Jacks, and from the centre of the engine rose an arch wreathed with flowers and evergreens surmounted by the Prince of Wales Feathers.' The original No 21 was built by Sharp Stewart for passenger traffic in 1864, and the 0-6-0 tank engine, which inherited the number in 1910, was built by Kitson of Leeds. This locomotive was renumbered 57 in 1918 and was scrapped in 1932 as LMS number 12502.

The single line in the foreground was a private siding that served the works of the Furness Chemical Company, and a spare section of bridge track can be seen lying on the ground between the running line and the siding. *5320*

Above The station at Haverthwaite, its main building almost identical to that at Greenodd, was approached at either end through a tunnel. In addition to its two passenger platforms, it had a goods shed, a weighbridge and a goods yard extensive enough to deal with the freight traffic generated by the nearby iron, gunpowder and dye-making industries. In this photograph 2-4-2 tank engine No 74 enters with a passenger train from Lakeside. Like Greenodd, Haverthwaite was closed to passenger traffic in 1946, but the goods yard continued in use until the demise of the Backbarrow Iron Works brought about complete closure of the Lakeside branch on 24 April 1967, passengers services to Lakeside having already been withdrawn on 6 September 1965.

However, not only has Haverthwaite station and yard survived, having been acquired in 1970 by the Lakeside & Haverthwaite Railway, but passenger services are once again operating, after a section of the line, from Haverthwaite to Lakeside, was re-opened on 2 May 1973 following a ceremony performed by the late Bishop Eric Treacy. *4008*

Below Map of Haverthwaite station. *Mike Faulkner*

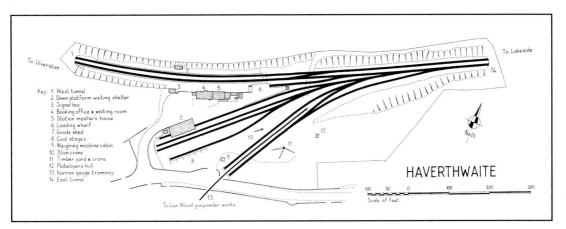

Key: 1. West tunnel
2. Down platform waiting shelter
3. Signal box
4. Booking office & waiting room
5. Station master's house
6. Loading wharf
7. Goods shed
8. Coal stages
9. Weighing machine cabin
10. 3 ton crane
11. Timber yard & crane
12. Platelayers hut
13. Narrow gauge tramway
14. East tunnel

To Ulverston

To Lakeside

North

HAVERTHWAITE

Scale of feet.

To Low Wood gunpowder works

Above The original intention was for the Lakeside branch to terminate at Newby Bridge, but before the building of the line was complete a decision was made to extend to Lakeside. The steamer landing at Newby Bridge was seen to be inadequate for operating the larger, deeper-draught steamers envisaged by the Railway Company to foster tourist traffic on the branch line, while extension to Lakeside would enable a combined railway station and steamer wharf, capable of accommodating the new steamers, to be sited at the foot of the lake.

It is interesting to note that on 19 August 1903 proposals were discussed by the Furness Railway Board to electrify the Lakeside branch, power being supplied either by a steam generating station, or by harnessing the waters of the nearby fast-flowing River Leven. It was decided, however, that the cost of this would be prohibitive, and a further proposal to introduce a steam railmotor car, which could run on both the Lakeside and Coniston branches, was adopted instead. The railmotor, which could carry 12 1st Class and 36 3rd Class passengers, also had a trailer, with seating for a further 24 3rd Class passengers, available for use as required. Built by the Railway Company in its Barrow workshops at a cost of £2,000, the railmotor was ready to enter service at the start of the 1905 summer timetable. In preparation for this event a timber platform was built at Newby Bridge to allow passengers wishing to alight there to do so without having to walk back from Lakeside. The new station was known as Newby Bridge Motor Car Platform, and photographs exist of it carrying that name.

It is on record that during May 1905, 198 passengers alighted from the railmotor at Newby Bridge and 52

had booked from there. Despite early promise, however, the railmotor was not a success and it was withdrawn from service on the Lakeside branch at the end of the 1905 season, although it continued to run on the Coniston branch until the end of the 1908 Winter timetable, much to the aggravation of the regular passengers on that line who complained frequently about the uncomfortable ride of the vehicle. Newby Bridge station was, however, kept in operation, although it was necessary to lengthen the platform in order to accommodate ordinary trains. This work was carried out during the winter of 1905-06, and at the same time the name was changed to Newby Bridge Platform, as seen on this photograph.

Note the signal beyond the platform, operated from the ground frame at the near end of the waiting shelter by passengers wishing to join trains. Newby Bridge Platform was closed to passenger traffic in 1939, although it was used during the war in connection with the transport of prisoners-of-war to nearby Grizedale Hall. Re-opened by

the Lakeside & Haverthwaite Railway in 1973, the platform building had by that time been removed and has since been replaced by a bus-type shelter provided by members of the Lakeside Railway Society, whose intention it is eventually to build a replica of the original waiting shelter. *2390*

Below left A passenger train headed by 2-4-2 tank engine No 71 running bunker first enters Newby Bridge Platform on its way to Lakeside. In the foreground is a Furness Railway platform seat with the distinctive 'squirrel and grapes' ends. Painted red in urban areas and with alternate red and cream slats on rural stations, the seats usually had the station name painted on the top rail of the back-rest. As stations closed, or became unstaffed, during the 1960s, the seats were removed and sold to enthusiasts, sometimes for as little as 2s 6d. *4905*

Above This view from a departing steamer shows to advantage the combined station and landing pier at Lakeside. The refreshment pavilion was not always as extensive as it is shown here, originally occupying only some 60 feet in the centre of the wharf. By 1906, however, the accommodation was becoming inadequate to deal with the number of passengers wishing to use it, and managers Spiers & Pond submitted a claim for enlargement of the premises, stating that during the period 1 June to 17 August they had provided 836 breakfasts, 4,305 lunches and 3,551 teas, it being necessary, on several occasions, to set up tables on the landing stage to provide the extra accommodation needed to serve this number of meals. The Railway Company agreed to extend the pavilion by a further 50 feet in the northerly direction in time for the 1907 season. Up to this time, too, the veranda had been open-sided and attention was drawn to the discomfort

Lakeside Pavilion

Under the Management of the Furness Railway Co.	Accommodation for Parties up to 300.	Adjoining Station and Steamer Pier.

Hot & Cold Luncheons, 2/6
DAILY, from 11-30 a.m. to 2-30 p.m.

Afternoon Teas - - 1/3
FROM 3 TO 6 P.M.

SPLENDID VIEWS OF WINDERMERE LAKE AND SURROUNDING HILLS.

For Terms and Particulars, apply to
MANAGERESS, REFRESHMENT PAVILION,
LAKESIDE (Windermere),
Via ULVERSTON.

suffered by diners from smoke and soot due to the close proximity of steamer funnels, with rain also blowing in on wet days. Once again the Railway Company responded, the Board authorising the installation of rolling glass screens at a cost of £150 at its meeting on 30 October 1906. There is still an overhead refreshment room at Lakeside station and it still contains some of the original ironwork, but its size has been reduced to approximately that of the 1906 season.

The steamer still alongside is *Swift*, while on the right of the picture can be seen the stern and vertical boiler of the barge *Raven*. *5216*

THE FURNESS RAILWAY

Left An interior view of the veranda refreshment pavilion, complete with hanging baskets, under which are posed the members of Bateson's Orchestral Band, a small locally based ensemble that played daily during the summer season for the enjoyment of passengers using the dining room, and occasionally on the lake steamers. Organised by Mr Thomas Bateson of Bowness, who played the cornet, he was supported by his wife, seated in front of him, who played the violin. The harpist was Mr Nightingale from Ely, Mr Booth from Accrington played the flute and Mr Walker of Shipley performed on the double bass. The name of the clarinettist is not known. Started by Mr Bateson's father in 1859, the band entertained Furness Railway passengers continuously until the end of the 1915 summer season, but the Railway Company Board, at its meeting on 9 May 1916, decided not to continue the practice because of the war, despite protestations from Mr Bateson that none of his players were eligible for military service. *5715*

Stank branch

The Stank branch came into operation in 1873 to serve the mines opened at this quaintly named Furness village just to the east of Barrow, after the discovery of iron ore deposits nearby. During building, the earthworks were

Mining continued at Stank until 1901 when the mines were closed and the branch line reduced to the short siding seen in this photograph, which would have been taken some time after 1925, as the single-decker bus in the background, on its way to Rampside, is one of five supplied in that year by Guy Motors for use on the coast road route between Barrow and Ulverston. The wagons are standing at Fishers Sand siding, the only use of the truncated branch for many

Below left When it was first built, the terminal station of the Lakeside branch, with its yellow bricks and black banding, was considered by many local residents as being too striking, in contrast to the grey Lakeland stone buildings nearby. It was nevertheless, with its steeply roofed tower, an imposing building, officially described as being in an Italianate style of architecture. It had, in addition to its imposing frontage, considerable facilities for the terminus of a branch line aimed primarily at the tourist trade. The train shed, which had direct access to the steamer landing, housed two platforms served by three roads, and the overhead refreshment veranda gave diners an unrivalled view of Windermere Lake; there was also a goods shed, an engine shed with turntable and a water tower.

Closed when passenger services were withdrawn on the branch on 6 September 1965, this fine building lay derelict until it was declared unsafe because of dry rot, and demolished a few months before acquisition of the site by the Lakeside & Haverthwaite Railway. *4918*

constructed for double track, since at the time there was a proposal, never realised, to build a railway line from Salthouse, through the low Furness villages of Gleaston and Urswick, to rejoin the main line beyond Lindal. In the event only the 2 miles from Salthouse to Stank were ever built.

years. Also in the background can be seen the two rows of terraced sandstone cottages built at Roose between 1873 and 1875 to house Cornish miners, working at Stank, who had moved north in search of employment in the booming Furness mining industry. Known as North and South Rows, the cottages still exist in much the same form as they were built some 120 years ago. *D623*

Piel branch

The line to Rampside and Piel was one of the original sections of the 1846 Furness Railway, leaving the route to Barrow and the iron ore jetties at a junction just south of Roose. It was built to form a connection with steamer services across Morecambe Bay to Fleetwood, operated by a banker, John Abel Smith, who in 1843 had purchased Roa Island. Here he built a jetty, extending into deep water, for use by his steamers, at the same time joining the island to the mainland by means of an embankment capable of carrying a railway.

The Furness Company negotiated rights to operate trains on a line built over the causeway, but by some oversight did not gain access to the steamer pier. Differences between Smith and the Railway Company on this issue led to another pier being built by the Railway Company at Barrow, but this was dependant upon tides, a disadvantage which the Roa Island jetty did not have. The situation became so difficult that the Company entered into negotiations with Smith to lease the embankment, together with Roa Island and its pier, but on 27 December 1852 nature intervened when a great storm severely damaged both pier and causeway. Smith, unwilling to face the high cost of repairs, sold out all his holdings to the Furness Company for the sum of £15,000.

Below The Piel branch Summer timetable of 1914 shows five trains in each direction daily, with extra services on Thursdays and Saturdays.

PIEL BRANCH.

DOWN.	1	2 (A)	3	4	5	6	7 (B)
	a m	a m	p m	p m	p m	p m	p m
Barrow Central...dep	8 5	11 15	12 35	2 30	5 55	8 25	10 45
Rampside .... ,,	8 14	11 24	12 44	2 39	6 4	8 34	10 54
Piel.....................afr	8 17	11 27	12 47	2 42	6 7	8 37	10 57

UP.	1	2 (A)	3	4	5	6	7 (B)
	a m	a m	p m	p m	p m	p m	p m
Piel ....dep	8 23	11 33	1 28	2 48	6 13	8 43	11 3
Rampside .... ,,	8 26	11 36	1 31	2 51	6 16	8 46	11 6
Barrow Central...arr	8 35	11 45	1 40	3 0	6 25	8 55	11 15

A—Saturdays only. B—Thursdays and Saturdays only, and on August Bank Holiday.

Bottom left Salthouse Halt, the small platform seen here, was situated on a curve opened in 1873 that left the Barrow-bound line at Salthouse Junction and joined the Rampside section at Parrock Hall Junction. Built after the First World War, and opened on 22 May 1920, the need for a halt between Barrow and Roose had first been raised by residents of Salthouse as early as 21 January 1909, but the Railway Company's Board deferred the request at the time and finally rejected it on 1 July 1910. The reason for its eventual building on the Piel branch, between Barrow and Rampside, is obscure, but it had its own booking office, which is the small

flat-topped wooden hut seen beyond the right-hand crossing gate. The crossing itself admitted vehicular traffic into Barrow's 1917-opened Salthouse Gas Works. *6000*

Above right Situated at the mainland end of the causeway to Roa Island, the station at Rampside was known originally as Concle station; a nearby inn still carries the name Concle, and it was not renamed Rampside station until 1869. The platform, initially only 192 feet long, was extended to 500 feet in 1911, following delays at the station

on Whit Monday of that year when 2,400 passengers were booked, and the short platform made ticket collecting difficult. During the summer of 1920 a special Saturday afternoon train ran taking passengers from Salthouse Halt to Rampside. Closed to passengers on 6 July 1936, the station and station house, the building on the left of the line, can still be recognised, and traces of the platform can still be found. *6984*

Below Map of Piel station, Roa Island. *Mike Faulkner*

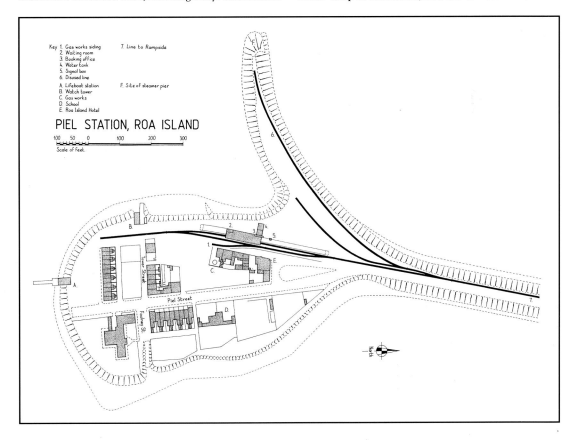

Key 1. Gas works siding
2. Waiting room
3. Booking office
4. Water tank
5. Signal box
6. Disused line
A. Lifeboat station
B. Watch tower
C. Gas works
D. School
E. Roa Island Hotel
7. Line to Rampside
F. Site of steamer pier

PIEL STATION, ROA ISLAND

100 50 0   100   200   300
Scale of Feet.

THE FURNESS RAILWAY

Left Seen from the pilot's watch tower ('B' in the plan opposite) this picture of Piel station tells much of the story of the railway to Roa Island. The train in the station is hauled by 2-4-0 locomotive No 75, one of a number of similar passenger engines built for the Furness Railway by Sharp Stewart (this one in 1872). No 75 was one of the engines converted to 2-4-2 tank locomotives in 1897, which gives some indication of the date of the picture; she was scrapped in 1914. The train has just crossed John Abel Smith's embankment joining the Island and the mainland in the background. Beyond the water tank (on the left of the station) can be seen the curve that carried the original line to Piel Pier and steamers to Belfast, while on the right, served by a short spur, is the Furness Railway's gas works, which produced the gas needed on the island and to illuminate the buoys marking the navigable channel into the port of Barrow.

The branch closed on 6 July 1936, only a short spur to the Salthouse gas works being retained, which was extended in 1954 to serve the new Barrow Electricity Generating Station at Roosecote. There is now no trace that the railway ever existed at Roa Island, and only the Hotel can still be recognised. *Author's collection*

Below left A 2-4-0 passenger engine, No 46, having discharged its passengers at Piel station, is running round the train in preparation for the tender-first return trip to Barrow. Built by Sharp Stewart in 1872, No 46 was scrapped in 1920. The Roa Island gas works, which closed on 31 March 1922, is on the right. The Piel branch service was known affectionately to locals as the 'Piel Nag'. *Author's collection*

Below Although situated on Roa Island, the terminal station of the branch was known as Piel station. Steamer services from Piel Pier continued until 1882, at which time they were transferred to the newly constructed steamer berths in Walney Channel, adjacent to the entrance to Ramsden Dock, and, direct boat trains to the island no longer being needed, the section of line between Roose and Parrock Hall junctions was taken out, thereafter only local services from Barrow being operated. After falling into decay, the pier was finally demolished. As can be seen from the photograph and the plan opposite, the station was a very simple affair, consisting of a single platform partially covered by a short train shed. A loop line, running outside the shed, allowed engines to run round their trains, and a short siding served the gas works, there being no mains gas on Roa Island until the Salthouse Gas Works was opened in 1917. Movement of engines and trains was controlled from a small signal box on the platform, opened on 15 October 1900, which after closure of the branch became a ground frame box at the north end of Barrow Central station. *6990*

Coniston branch

Broughton was, until 1858, the junction station between the Furness Railway extending northwards from Barrow and the Whitehaven & Furness Junction Railway coming south from Whitehaven. In that year the two systems were linked by the installation of a curve at Foxfield, opened on 1 August, which eliminated the need for through trains to run into Broughton, and the interchange was transferred to a newly built station at Foxfield (see page 53).

The year 1859, however, saw Broughton regain its interchange function with the arrival of the Coniston Railway, a line built principally to transport minerals mined at Coniston, which hitherto had been carried in barges along Coniston Lake for shipping from the small port of Greenodd. The line also had a tourist potential in connection with the steam yacht *Gondola*, which had commenced pleasure sailings on the lake in the same year. Although not initially part of the Furness Railway, the line was built with that Company's assistance, its directors also served on the Furness Board, and the Furness supplied all motive power and stock used on the railway prior to its amalgamation with the parent company in 1862. Passenger traffic commenced on the branch on 18 June 1859, but it was to be another year before mineral traffic began.

Below This view of Broughton station, taken from an elevated position to the east, shows the village beyond and Dunnerdale Fell dominant in the background. The station illustrated dates from the opening of the Coniston branch; the original, which would have been situated about on the new trackbed, was demolished to make way for the new line. On 8 July 1903 a second offset wooden platform with loop, seen on the left of the photograph, was brought into use at a cost of £1,000. This allowed two trains to cross without the need for one of them to be shunted into the goods yard. Later in the same year a further £250 was expended on extensions to the waiting rooms in the main building. In the centre of this picture a line of Furness Railway wagons stands in front of the goods shed, which itself is partially obscuring the 1903 extensions to the waiting rooms. *5446*

Right Another view of Broughton station, seen from the wooden platform. The signal box, just visible in the background, opened on 31 May 1897 when the branch was re-signalled to comply with the 1889 Regulations of Railways Act. The station closed in 1958 but still exists as two private dwellings. 2532

Below right The line from Broughton to Coniston was single track and had two intermediate stations at Woodland and Torver. Woodland, like Broughton, had two platforms with a passing loop, and the station building was also the Post Office. Pictured in the late 1950s, with a push-pull train from Coniston on its way to Broughton, the passing loop can clearly be seen. Woodland's station buildings still exist as a private dwelling, preserved almost as they were in Furness Railway days with both platforms and all buildings except the signal box still standing. *Author's collection*

Left Torver had its passing loop taken out in 1897, thereafter having only a single track with a goods shed and goods wharf sited just south of the station, controlled by a ground frame. As at Woodland, Torver's station building still exists as a private dwelling and is still recognisable. The goods shed is also still standing, having been renovated and re-roofed following fire damage some years ago. The trackbed to the goods wharf and beyond has been incorporated into improvements to the A593 road between Coniston and Broughton. *2756*

Below left Another view of Torver station from the road bridge carrying the A5084 road over the railway to meet the A593 Broughton to Coniston road, clearly showing the site of the loop. The station wears a neglected air, which is not surprising as it was photographed in August 1958, just a few weeks before passenger services were withdrawn. *A. L. Headech collection*

Coniston Branch and Lake Steamers with Connections. 4

DOWN.	Week Days.													Sundays.			
	1	2	3	4	5	6	7	8	9	10	11	12	13	1	2	3	4
	a m	a m	a m	a m	p m		p m	p m	p m		p m	p m	p m	a m	p m	p m	
Carnforth ....dep	..	7 0	..	9 50	1215	..	1 25	3 48	4 0	..	..	6 20		7 35	..	..	..
Grange ....,,	..	7 25	..	9 55	1231	..	1 50	4 4	4 30	..	..	6 45		8 0	..	..	..
Ulverston ....,,	..	7 52	..	1032	1248	..	2 17	4 21	4 57	..	..	7 12		8 27	1 32	6 22	..
Dalton ....,,	..	8 5	..	1035	1259	..	2 30	4 20	5 10	..	..	7 25		8 40	1 45	6 35	..
Furness Abbey .....,,	..	8 10	..	1040	1 4	..	2 35	4 25	5 15	..	..	7 30		8 45	1 50	6 40	..
Barrow ((Dock) .....,,	..	6 45	..	..	12 5	..	..	..	..	..	..	6 10		..	..	6 10	..
((Central) ....,,	..	8 25	..	1110	1 17	..	2 50	4 45	5 40	..	..	7 45		9 0	2 30	6 55	..
Whitehaven, Bransty..,,	6 40	6 40	..	1015	1140	L	1 30	3 35	..	..	5 40	5 40	7e30	8 30	..	5 40	..
Millom ....,,	7 55	7 55	9 0	1130	1241		2 45	4 50	..	..	6 55	6 55	9 5	9 45	..	6 55	..
FOXFIELD ....dep	8 14	8 55	9 20	1155	1 40	..	3 20	5 10	6 25	..	7 10	8 15	9 20	10 0	2 57	7 25	..
Broughton............,,	8 18	9 0	9 23	1159	1 45	..	3 23	5 13	6 30	..	7 13	8 18	9 23	10 33	0 7	7 28	..
Woodland ....,,	..	9 8	..	12 7	1 53	..	3 30	5 20	6 38	..	---	8 25	9 30	1010	3	7 35	..
Torver ....,,	..	9 19	..	1214	2 4	..	3 37	5 28	6 49	..	..	8 32	9 38	1018	3 18	7 43	..
CONISTON ....arr	..	9 25	9 40	1220	2 10	..	3 45	5 35	6 55	..	..	8 40	9 45	1025	3 25	7 50	..

A Tuesdays, Thursdays and Saturdays only.   **E** Passengers change at Millom.   **F** Daily until September 19th, and afterwards Thursdays and Saturdays only.   **L** Leaves Whitehaven 11-25 a.m. and Millom 12-26 p.m. until July 11th.

For other connections see page 1.

UP.	Week Days.												Sundays.			
	1	2	3	4	5	6	7	8	9	10	11	12	1	2	3	4
	a m	a m	a m	a m	a m		p m	p m	p m	p m	p m	p m	a m	p m	p m	
CONISTON ....dep	7 30	..	8 40	11 5	1150	..	2 25	4 15	6 0	6 25	..	8*45	9 0	3 58	8 0	..
Torver ....,,	7 37	..	8 46	1111	1157	..	2 31	4 22	..	6 31	..	8*51	9 6	6 41	8 6	..
Woodland ....,,	7 48	..	8 54	1119	12 8	..	2 39	4 33	..	6 39	..	8*59	9 14	6 49	8 14	..
Broughton............,,	7 56	8 41	9 2	1127	1216	..	2 47	4 41	6 17	6 47	7 52	9* 7	9 22	6 57	8 22	..
FOXFIELD ....arr	8 0	8 45	9 5	1130	1220	..	2 50	4 45	6 20	6 50	7 55	9*10	9 25	7 0	8 25	..
Millom ....arr	9 3	9 3	..	1148	1 48	..	3 31	5 2	6 35	8 23	8 23	11*38	9 41	7 36	..	..
Whitehaven, Bransty ..,,	10 7	10 7	..	1 5	2 53	..	4 45	6 17	7 38	9 55	9 55	..	1055	8 50	..	..
Barrow ((Central) ...,,	8 35	..	9 40	1210	1 10	F	3 25	5 30	6 42	7 35	..	9*45	1025	7 35	8 55	..
((Dock) .....,,	8 45	..	..	..	1 55	H	..	6 55	8 25	..	..	..	1040	7 50	..	..
Furness Abbey ....,,	8 50	..	9 53	1230	1 20	K	3 45	5 50	7 0	7 50	..	10*18	1045	7 55	..	..
Dalton ....,,	8 55	..	9 58	1235	2 5	..	3 50	5 57	5 7	7 55	..	10*22	1058	8	..	..
Ulverston ....,,	9 8	..	1011	1248	1 37		4 3	6 8	7 15	8	..	11*25	5 37	8 32	..	..
Grange ....,,	9 37	..	1035	1 12	1 55	F	4 27	6 32	7 35	8 32	..	---	5	..	..	..
Carnforth ....,,	10 5	..	11 0	1 40	2 12		4 55	7 0	7 52	9 0	..	..	6 59	0	..	..

A Tuesdays, Thursdays and Saturdays only.   **F** Until July 11th will arrive Barrow 12-55, Ulverston 1-18, Grange 2-42, and Carnforth 1-47 p.m.   **H** Daily until Sept. 19th, and afterwards on Thursdays and Saturdays only.   **K** Commencing July 13th stops to set down from Coniston Branch on informing the Guard at Barrow.   * Saturdays till Sept. 19th only.   † Commencing July 13th.

For other connections see page 1.

CONISTON LAKE STEAMERS.

DOWN.	WEEK DAYS.							
	1	2	3	4	5	6	7	8
	E		E			E	F	G E
	a m	a m	noon	p m		p m	p m	p m p m
Waterhead..dep	10 15	11 35	12 0	12 55	..	1 20	2 45	3 10 4 30
Lake Bank ..arr	10 50	12 10	12 35	1 30	..	1 55	3 20	3 45 5 5

UP.	WEEK DAYS.							
	1	2	3	4	5	6	7	8
	E		E			E	F	G E
	a m	p m	p m	p m	p m	p m	p m	p m p m
Lake Bank ..dep	10 55	12 15	12 40	1 35	2 0	3 25	3 50	5 10
Waterhead ..arr	11 30	12 50	1 15	2 10	2 35	4 0	4 25	5 45

E Till August 31st only.   **F** 30 mts. earlier during September.   **G** 25 mts. later during September.

A Steam Yacht will make the Tour of the Lake on Sundays, leaving Waterhead at 2-0, 4-15 and 5-30 p.m.

The Coniston branch and lake steamer services, from the Summer timetable of 1914.

Above The Coniston station seen here dates from 1862, but presumably a station of some sort existed before that, the line having been opened three years earlier, although nothing is known of that structure. Designed by Edward Paley, in a 'Swiss chalet' style of architecture that fitted in with the surrounding mountain scenery, the station was enlarged in 1888 and again in about 1896, this time by the addition of another platform, extension of the existing covered platforms and a new signal box.

The three platforms all appear in this photograph of the southern end of the train shed, together with the entrance to an integral goods shed, just visible to the left of the footbridge. Beyond the station at the northern end was a single-track spur, opened in 1860, which ran to Coppermines Wharf to facilitate the conveyance of copper ore from the mines on the slopes of Coniston Old Man.

Having opened on 18 June 1859, the branch closed to passenger traffic on 6 October 1958. Thereafter a three-times-weekly goods train ran until this too was withdrawn on 30 April 1962, at which time complete closure of the line from Foxfield to Coniston took place. Coniston station was demolished a year or two later after being vandalised. The footbridge, however, has survived and now helps passengers negotiate the tracks at today's 15-inch-gauge railway station at Ravenglass, while part of the frame from the signal box is installed in the box at Park South near Barrow. *6850*

Below left In this similar view, a little to the right and looking across the railway in an easterly direction towards the village, the signal box, which was brought from Carnforth F&M junction when Coniston station was enlarged in 1896, can be seen on the left of the picture standing on its local stone plinth with weighbridge and stone-built weigh office. The diverging track beyond the signal box led to a single-road engine shed with turntable, in which the branch engine was stored overnight, in order to be available to operate the early morning passenger service to Foxfield. The shed and turntable fell out of use when British Railways introduced motor-fitted trains, which did not require the engine to be switched to the front of the train for the return journey. There was another, much smaller signal box, housing a ground frame, at the northern end of the station, and this has survived to be installed in a private garden railway in Coniston village. *6851*

Although taken in 1939, this comprehensive view of Coniston station provides an evocative look at the scene as it would have been in Furness Railway days. Apart from the LMS coaches in the platform, a couple of LMS wagons and a motor lorry emerging from the goods shed, little has changed. Note the Furness Railway signals, the hand-operated yard crane, two wagons of loco coal in the foreground and a private owner wagon. The station forecourt too, with its porch and horse-drawn vehicles, is reminiscent of an earlier time. *Authors' collection*

Bardsea branch

Acts of Parliament dated 27 June 1876 and 11 August 1881 authorised the building of the Bardsea branch, intended originally as a double track loop line from the main line at Plumpton Junction to Barrow, thus avoiding the very busy Lindal area and also saving some of the expense of banking heavy trains up the steeply graded section of line between Ulverston and Lindal Ore Sidings.

In the event only 2 miles of track were constructed, crossing the Ulverston Canal on an opening bridge and terminating at Priory station, just short of Bardsea, the village from which the branch took its name. Earthworks were built for a few hundred yards beyond the station, which are still recognisable, but the loop line scheme was abandoned before the line had progressed any further. Opened for traffic on 27 June 1883, with two mixed trains per day in each direction, the journey from Ulverston was timetabled to take 12 minutes. By 1886 passenger services had been reduced to one train per day, at lunchtime, and in 1916, as a wartime economy measure, the line was reduced to single track between the North Lonsdale crossing and Priory station. The rails released by this action were reputedly used for additional sidings at Barrow. Passenger services were withdrawn on 6 March 1916.

Below The principal industrial site served by the branch was the North Lonsdale Ironworks, opened in 1874 and financed by a large group of investors, of which the well-known local Ainslie and Kennedy families were the major shareholders. Until the advent of the Bardsea branch the works relied for its railway connection on a siding that ran to a paper mill on the side of the Ulverston Canal. The works had four smelting furnaces, of which only two were in blast at any one time; the sheerlegs at the top of the right-hand furnace suggest that this was being relined at the time of the photograph. Wagons from several companies can be identified, including Westwood Coke Ovens (marked 'WW'), Grange Colliery, Yorkshire (marked 'G'), and North Eastern Railway, and they are being marshalled by what appears to be a rebuilt Sharp Stewart 0-6-0 locomotive of the Furness Railway. The loaded wagons were lifted to the high-level platform by the hoist on the left; once there they discharged their loads of iron ore, coke

and limestone, the raw materials of iron production, into the various storage bins beneath, before being returned to ground level by the hoist on the right. The ironworks closed in 1938, although a foundry continued in production until after the war and the site was cleared some time after 1945. In 1948 Glaxo Laboratories (now Glaxo Wellcome) moved in and commenced to build the present plant, continuing to work the truncated branch for several years, using their own diesel locomotive latterly, but the last train ran on 27 April 1994. The track is expected to be lifted by the time this book is published. *3560*

Top The short Bardsea Branch could boast only two railway-orientated buildings, North Lonsdale Crossing signal box, which controlled a level crossing, traffic into the ironworks and trains to Priory station, and Priory station itself. The signal box closed on 2 August 1938 and was demolished during the 1960s, but the station building still stands and is easily recognisable, even though it is now a private residence. The red-brick building, designed by Paley and Austin, had toilets, ladies and general waiting rooms,

ticket office, Station Master's house, and a single platform with a run-around, allowing trains to be hauled in both directions, more than adequate facilities considering it never had more than two trains per day. The station was always grossly underused and closed when passenger services were withdrawn on 6 March 1916. This photograph is dated December 1958 and the station nameboard is still in place, more than 42 years after closure, but this has now gone, to be preserved in a private collection. *A. L. Headech*

Above Priory station as it is in 2001. Now known as South Lodge House, the building has been luxuriously converted into a very desirable self-catering holiday cottage. The exterior is still easily recognisable from the 1958 picture, the major differences being the replacement of the toilet and coal store block, on the extreme left, by an elegant conservatory, and the conversion of the rough ground in front of the building into a tennis court and putting green. The platform has been retained as a paved terrace, and Furness Railway buffer stops were discovered during restoration. *R. F. Fisher*

Conishead Priory, the magnificent pile after which Priory station was named, has had a varied existence since its foundation as a hospital and Augustinian priory in the 12th century. Following the dissolution of the monasteries in the 16th century it was sold by the Crown for conversion into a private residence, passing eventually into the ownership of the wealthy local Bradyll family. It was Colonel Thomas Bradyll who, in the 1820s, demolished the original house and rebuilt it in the splendid Gothic style seen here. When the Bradyll family fortune failed the Priory was sold again, by auction, and became a Hydropathic Hotel, served for a time at least by its own railway station. However, the rail service was so inadequate that as early as 1901 it had an omnibus service to and from Ulverston station for the benefit of guests, as can be seen from the accompanying advertisement from a Tourist Guide of 1901. Listed in the 1927 Automobile Association Handbook as a four-star establishment with 126 bedrooms, the Priory was sold once more in 1929 to the Durham Mineworkers' Welfare Committee to become a convalescent and rest home for miners. Thus it remained until 1967 and during this time the Sankey photographers paid fortnightly visits to take pictures of the current patients. This photograph was probably taken during one of these visits, and the presence of the Sankey bull-nosed Morris Cowley motor car on the forecourt dates the scene as the late 1930s.

Following the departure of the miners the building stood empty for nearly ten years, during which time it began to fall into dereliction until the present owners, the Manjushri Institute, moved in to establish a Buddhist Centre and immediately took steps to halt the decay. That was in 1976, and astonishing progress has been made to restore the Priory to its former splendour. E17

INDEX